BLUE TEAM OPERATIONS

DEFENSE

OPERATONAL SECURITY, INCIDENT RESPONSE & DIGITAL FORENSICS

4 BOOKS IN 1

BOOK 1
BLUE TEAM ESSENTIALS: A BEGINNER'S GUIDE TO OPERATIONAL SECURITY

BOOK 2
MASTERING INCIDENT RESPONSE: STRATEGIES FOR BLUE TEAMS

BOOK 3
DIGITAL FORENSICS FOR BLUE TEAMS: ADVANCED TECHNIQUES AND INVESTIGATIONS

BOOK 4
EXPERT BLUE TEAM OPERATIONS: DEFENDING AGAINST ADVANCED THREATS

ROB BOTWRIGHT

Published by Rob Botwright
Library of Congress Cataloging-in-Publication Data
ISBN 978-1-83938-561-2
Cover design by Rizzo

Disclaimer

The contents of this book are based on extensive research and the best available historical sources. However, the author and publisher make no claims, promises, or guarantees about the accuracy, completeness, or adequacy of the information contained herein. The information in this book is provided on an "as is" basis, and the author and publisher disclaim any and all liability for any errors, omissions, or inaccuracies in the information or for any actions taken in reliance on such information.

The opinions and views expressed in this book are those of the author and do not necessarily reflect the official policy or position of any organization or individual mentioned in this book. Any reference to specific people, places, or events is intended only to provide historical context and is not intended to defame or malign any group, individual, or entity. The information in this book is intended for educational and entertainment purposes only. It is not intended to be a substitute for professional advice or judgment. Readers are encouraged to conduct their own research and to seek professional advice where appropriate.

Every effort has been made to obtain necessary permissions and acknowledgments for all images and other copyrighted material used in this book. Any errors or omissions in this regard are unintentional, and the author and publisher will correct them in future editions.

TABLE OF CONTENTS – BOOK 1 - BLUE TEAM ESSENTIALS: A BEGINNER'S GUIDE TO OPERATIONAL SECURITY

TABLE OF CONTENTS – BOOK 2 - MASTERING INCIDENT RESPONSE: STRATEGIES FOR BLUE TEAMS

TABLE OF CONTENTS – BOOK 3 - DIGITAL FORENSICS FOR BLUE TEAMS: ADVANCED TECHNIQUES AND INVESTIGATIONS

TABLE OF CONTENTS – BOOK 4 - EXPERT BLUE TEAM OPERATIONS: DEFENDING AGAINST ADVANCED THREATS

Introduction

Welcome to the world of "Blue Team Operations: Defense" –
a comprehensive book bundle that equips you with the
knowledge and skills needed to excel in the realm of
cybersecurity defense. In an era where cyber threats loom
large and the stakes have never been higher, the role of blue
teams in safeguarding digital assets and information systems
is paramount. This book bundle, comprising four distinct
volumes, explores operational security, incident response,
digital forensics, and advanced threat defense, offering a
holistic approach to protecting your organization's digital
landscape.

Book 1 - Blue Team Essentials: A Beginner's Guide to
Operational Security
Our journey begins with "Blue Team Essentials: A Beginner's
Guide to Operational Security," where we lay the
foundational principles of operational security. In this
volume, we guide you through the fundamental concepts of
threat assessment, risk management, and secure
communication practices. Whether you're new to the world
of cybersecurity or seeking to refresh your knowledge, this
book provides an accessible entry point into the critical field
of blue team operations.

Book 2 - Mastering Incident Response: Strategies for Blue
Teams
Moving forward, "Mastering Incident Response: Strategies
for Blue Teams" takes center stage. Here, we delve deep into
the art of incident response, teaching you how to develop
robust incident response plans, rapidly detect threats, and
orchestrate effective response strategies. With real-world

scenarios and expert guidance, you'll gain the skills needed to handle security incidents swiftly and decisively.

Book 3 - Digital Forensics for Blue Teams: Advanced Techniques and Investigations

In "Digital Forensics for Blue Teams: Advanced Techniques and Investigations," we enter the fascinating realm of digital forensics. This volume explores advanced methods for collecting and analyzing digital evidence, enabling you to conduct thorough investigations that uncover the truth behind security incidents. Whether you're dealing with cybercrime or insider threats, these advanced techniques will empower you to uncover the evidence needed for effective response and recovery.

Book 4 - Expert Blue Team Operations: Defending Against Advanced Threats

Our final destination, "Expert Blue Team Operations: Defending Against Advanced Threats," elevates your blue team capabilities to a whole new level. Here, we tackle the challenges posed by advanced adversaries, covering threat hunting, threat intelligence, and tactics for defending against the most sophisticated attacks. With insights from seasoned professionals, you'll be prepared to defend your organization against the ever-evolving threat landscape.

As you embark on this journey through "Blue Team Operations: Defense," you'll discover that the strength of the blue team lies not only in its technical expertise but also in its adaptability, collaboration, and commitment to continuous improvement. The knowledge and skills you gain from these volumes will not only enhance your individual capabilities but also contribute to the collective defense of organizations and institutions against cyber threats.

In an increasingly interconnected world, the mission of the blue team has never been more critical. We invite you to dive into this bundle and equip yourself with the tools, strategies, and insights necessary to become a defender of the digital realm. Whether you're a novice or a seasoned professional, "Blue Team Operations: Defense" has something valuable to offer you in the ever-evolving battle for cybersecurity.

BOOK 1
BLUE TEAM ESSENTIALS
A BEGINNER'S GUIDE TO OPERATIONAL SECURITY

ROB BOTWRIGHT

Chapter 1: Understanding Cyber Threats

Threat actors and their motivations lie at the heart of the complex cybersecurity landscape. These actors encompass a diverse spectrum, ranging from individual hackers to state-sponsored groups, each driven by distinct incentives and objectives. Understanding these motivations is pivotal in crafting effective defense strategies.

At one end of the spectrum, you have financially motivated cybercriminals seeking monetary gain through activities like ransomware attacks and credit card fraud. These individuals or groups often operate with the sole intent of profiting from their cyber exploits. Their motivations are primarily economic, aiming to maximize financial returns while minimizing risks.

On the other hand, there are hacktivists, who are motivated by ideological or political beliefs. They target organizations and institutions that they perceive as opposing their views or engaging in activities they find objectionable. Hacktivism can manifest as website defacement, distributed denial-of-service (DDoS) attacks, or data leaks intended to expose sensitive information.

State-sponsored threat actors represent another category with distinct motivations. Governments or government-affiliated groups engage in cyber espionage, cyber warfare, or cyber influence campaigns. Their objectives range from stealing intellectual property and military secrets to disrupting critical infrastructure and shaping global narratives. National interests and geopolitical considerations drive these actors.

Corporate espionage is another motivation that fuels cyber threats. Companies and competitors may engage in cyber-espionage to gain a competitive edge, access proprietary information, or sabotage rival businesses. The theft of trade secrets, research and development data, or strategic plans can be lucrative or strategically advantageous.

In contrast to these financially or politically driven motivations, there are cybercriminals who seek personal notoriety or thrill-seeking adventures. These individuals may engage in high-profile hacks or cyberattacks simply for the sake of gaining recognition within the hacking community or for the excitement of the challenge itself.

One motivation that transcends traditional boundaries is the lure of power. This can manifest in various ways, such as hacktivists striving to expose wrongdoing to assert moral authority or state-sponsored actors using cyber capabilities to extend their influence globally. The quest for power can be a potent driving force behind cyber threats.

Vandalism and disruption for the sake of causing chaos or destruction are motivations that might seem senseless, but they do exist within the threat landscape. Some attackers may derive satisfaction from disrupting services, causing system failures, or leaving a trail of digital destruction without any clear financial or ideological gain.

Furthermore, the dark web and underground cybercriminal forums play a pivotal role in shaping motivations. These platforms offer a thriving marketplace for stolen data, tools, and services, further fueling cybercrime. The anonymous nature of the internet and the potential for substantial financial rewards make these spaces attractive to various threat actors.

Motivations can evolve over time and may even overlap. For example, a financially motivated cybercriminal may inadvertently expose sensitive political information while seeking a ransom payment. Understanding these nuanced motivations is crucial for blue teams in the world of cybersecurity.

By comprehending the motivations of threat actors, defenders can better anticipate and prepare for potential attacks. Threat intelligence, including profiling and monitoring threat actors, helps organizations stay one step ahead by identifying emerging threats and adapting defense strategies accordingly.

Effective cybersecurity strategies involve a multifaceted approach that considers not only the technical aspects of defending against cyber threats but also the psychological and motivational factors that drive those threats. The ability to assess and adapt to changing motivations is a key element in the ongoing battle to protect digital assets and information.

In the ever-evolving landscape of cybersecurity, it's crucial to recognize the common cyber threats and attack vectors that pose risks to individuals, organizations, and even nations.

One prevalent threat is malware, a catch-all term encompassing various types of malicious software designed to infiltrate, disrupt, or steal data from target systems.

Viruses, one of the oldest forms of malware, replicate themselves by attaching to legitimate files and spreading when those files are executed.

Worms, on the other hand, don't need a host file and can propagate independently across networks, often with the goal of compromising vulnerable systems.

Trojans, named after the legendary wooden horse, disguise themselves as legitimate programs to deceive users into downloading and executing them, enabling unauthorized access or data theft.

Ransomware has gained notoriety in recent years as a particularly disruptive threat, encrypting victims' files and demanding a ransom for decryption keys.

Another common attack vector is phishing, where cybercriminals craft convincing emails or messages to trick recipients into revealing sensitive information like login credentials or financial details.

Spear phishing takes this a step further by customizing the attack for specific individuals or organizations, making it even more difficult to detect.

Social engineering attacks manipulate human psychology, often exploiting trust or urgency to trick victims into divulging information or performing actions they wouldn't otherwise do.

Distributed Denial of Service (DDoS) attacks flood a target's network or website with a massive volume of traffic, overwhelming it and rendering it inaccessible to users.

IoT devices, with their often lax security measures, have become attractive targets for attackers to compromise and use in DDoS attacks.

Zero-day vulnerabilities are software flaws unknown to the vendor, making them prime targets for exploitation.

Attackers who discover or purchase such vulnerabilities can develop exploits to breach systems before patches are available.

Advanced Persistent Threats (APTs) are highly sophisticated and targeted attacks, often associated with nation-states or well-funded cybercriminal groups.

These attackers operate quietly, infiltrating systems and maintaining access for extended periods, enabling data theft or espionage.

Brute force attacks involve systematically trying all possible combinations of passwords or encryption keys until the correct one is found.

Weak or easily guessable passwords are particularly vulnerable to this type of attack.

Man-in-the-Middle (MitM) attacks intercept communication between two parties, allowing the attacker to eavesdrop, modify, or inject malicious content.

Pharming attacks redirect website traffic to fraudulent sites without the user's knowledge, often used for phishing purposes.

Drive-by downloads occur when a user visits a compromised website that automatically initiates the download of malicious software to their device.

Cross-Site Scripting (XSS) attacks inject malicious scripts into web pages viewed by other users, potentially leading to the theft of their data or session cookies.

SQL injection attacks manipulate web application databases by inserting malicious SQL code into user inputs, potentially exposing sensitive data or compromising the application itself.

Watering hole attacks involve compromising websites that are likely to be visited by the target audience, such as employees of a specific company or members of an industry group.

Fileless malware operates in memory, leaving no trace on disk, making it challenging to detect and eradicate.

Cryptojacking is the unauthorized use of a victim's computing resources to mine cryptocurrency, slowing down the device and increasing energy costs.

Malvertising spreads malware through online ads, often on legitimate websites, exploiting vulnerabilities in the ad platform or user's browser.

Whaling attacks target high-profile individuals within organizations, such as CEOs or executives, with the goal of stealing sensitive information or financial assets.

Understanding these common cyber threats and attack vectors is essential for individuals and organizations to develop effective cybersecurity strategies and safeguard against potential risks.

By staying informed about the evolving threat landscape and implementing best practices in security, we can better protect our digital assets and information from cyberattacks.

Chapter 2: Introduction to Operational Security

Operational security, often abbreviated as OpSec, is a fundamental concept in the field of cybersecurity and risk management.

At its core, OpSec is about protecting sensitive information and safeguarding the confidentiality, integrity, and availability of assets.

In essence, it's the practice of mitigating risks by controlling the information that might be exploited by adversaries.

This discipline is not exclusive to the realm of cybersecurity; it extends to areas such as military operations, intelligence, and business continuity planning.

OpSec serves as a vital foundation for building comprehensive security strategies.

In today's interconnected world, where data flows seamlessly across networks and systems, operational security takes on even greater significance.

Whether you're an individual or part of an organization, understanding the basics of OpSec can help you make informed decisions about protecting sensitive information.

One fundamental principle of operational security is the need-to-know principle.

This principle dictates that individuals should only have access to information and resources necessary for their specific roles or tasks.

By limiting access in this way, you reduce the potential attack surface that malicious actors can exploit.

Another key concept in OpSec is risk assessment.

This involves identifying and evaluating potential risks to your operations, assets, and information.

Risk assessment helps you prioritize security measures and allocate resources effectively.

A crucial aspect of OpSec is information classification.

Different types of information have varying degrees of sensitivity, and it's essential to categorize and label them accordingly.

Typically, information is classified as public, internal use only, confidential, or highly classified, depending on its importance and the level of protection required.

To maintain operational security, you must implement access controls that align with the classification of information.

Access controls may include user authentication, encryption, and role-based access management.

These controls ensure that only authorized individuals can access sensitive information.

Regularly updating access permissions and revoking access for individuals who no longer require it is also part of OpSec best practices.

In addition to safeguarding information, physical security plays a significant role in OpSec.

Physical security measures protect facilities, equipment, and physical assets from unauthorized access, theft, or damage.

This might involve security cameras, access control systems, and security personnel.

Another critical component of OpSec is security awareness and training.

Educating individuals within an organization or group about security risks and best practices is essential.

Human error is a common cause of security breaches, so providing training can help prevent costly mistakes.

Phishing awareness training, for example, helps individuals recognize and avoid falling victim to phishing attacks.

An often-overlooked aspect of operational security is the proper disposal of sensitive information.

Physical documents, electronic storage media, and even old hardware can contain valuable data.

Failure to dispose of these items securely can lead to data breaches.

Secure disposal methods may include shredding, degaussing, or overwriting data on storage devices.

Incident response planning is a critical aspect of OpSec.

No matter how robust your security measures are, there's always a possibility of a security incident.

Having a well-defined incident response plan in place helps minimize the impact of an incident and ensures a swift and organized response.

This plan should outline the roles and responsibilities of the incident response team, procedures for reporting and documenting incidents, and steps for containing and mitigating threats.

Encryption is a powerful tool in operational security.

By encrypting sensitive data, even if it falls into the wrong hands, it remains unintelligible without the appropriate decryption key.

Encryption can be applied to data at rest, in transit, and in use.

It's a critical component of protecting data in scenarios like data breaches or theft of mobile devices.

Regularly updating and patching software and systems is a fundamental OpSec practice.

Many cyberattacks target known vulnerabilities in software and operating systems.

By keeping your systems up to date, you reduce the likelihood of falling victim to exploits that target outdated software.

Implementing a strong password policy is another OpSec measure that's often underestimated.

Weak passwords are a common entry point for attackers.

A robust password policy encourages the use of complex, unique passwords and enforces regular password changes.

Multi-factor authentication (MFA) is also a valuable addition to password security, providing an additional layer of protection.

OpSec extends to secure communication practices.

This includes using encrypted communication channels, especially when transmitting sensitive information.

Secure email protocols and encrypted messaging apps help protect the confidentiality of your communications.

Additionally, OpSec considers the risks posed by third-party vendors and partners.

When working with external entities, it's essential to evaluate their security practices and ensure they align with your OpSec requirements.

Failure to do so can introduce vulnerabilities into your operational environment.

It's important to remember that operational security is an ongoing process, not a one-time task.

As technology evolves and threats become more sophisticated, OpSec measures must adapt and evolve as well.

Regularly reviewing and updating your OpSec practices is essential to staying ahead of potential risks.

In summary, operational security is a comprehensive approach to protecting sensitive information and assets from a wide range of threats.

It encompasses principles such as need-to-know, risk assessment, information classification, access controls, physical security, security awareness, and encryption.

By implementing these principles and best practices, individuals and organizations can significantly enhance their security posture and minimize the risk of data breaches and other security incidents.

Operational security, often referred to as OpSec, is a critical aspect of safeguarding sensitive information and ensuring the security of systems and operations.

At its core, OpSec encompasses a set of principles and objectives aimed at mitigating risks and protecting against potential threats to an organization's mission and assets.

One of the fundamental principles of OpSec is the need-to-know principle, which dictates that individuals should only have access to information and resources necessary for their specific roles or tasks.

By adhering to this principle, organizations reduce the potential attack surface that malicious actors can exploit, limiting access to sensitive information.

Another key principle of OpSec is risk assessment.

This involves identifying and evaluating potential risks to an organization's operations, assets, and information.

Risk assessment helps organizations prioritize security measures and allocate resources effectively to address the most significant threats.

Information classification is another critical aspect of OpSec.

Different types of information have varying degrees of sensitivity, and it's essential to categorize and label them accordingly.

Typically, information is classified as public, internal use only, confidential, or highly classified, depending on its importance and the level of protection required.

To maintain operational security, organizations must implement access controls that align with the classification of information.

Access controls may include user authentication, encryption, and role-based access management.

These controls ensure that only authorized individuals can access sensitive information, preventing unauthorized access.

Regularly updating access permissions and revoking access for individuals who no longer require it is also part of OpSec best practices.

In addition to safeguarding information, physical security plays a significant role in OpSec.

Physical security measures protect facilities, equipment, and physical assets from unauthorized access, theft, or damage.

Security cameras, access control systems, and security personnel are some common components of physical security.

Security awareness and training are critical components of OpSec.

Educating individuals within an organization about security risks and best practices is essential.

Human error is a common cause of security breaches, so providing training can help prevent costly mistakes.

Phishing awareness training, for example, helps individuals recognize and avoid falling victim to phishing attacks.

Proper disposal of sensitive information is an often-overlooked aspect of operational security.

Physical documents, electronic storage media, and old hardware can contain valuable data.

Failure to dispose of these items securely can lead to data breaches.

Secure disposal methods may include shredding, degaussing, or overwriting data on storage devices.

Incident response planning is a critical aspect of OpSec.

No matter how robust an organization's security measures are, there's always a possibility of a security incident.

Having a well-defined incident response plan in place helps minimize the impact of an incident and ensures a swift and organized response.

This plan should outline the roles and responsibilities of the incident response team, procedures for reporting and documenting incidents, and steps for containing and mitigating threats.

Encryption is a powerful tool in operational security.

By encrypting sensitive data, even if it falls into the wrong hands, it remains unintelligible without the appropriate decryption key.

Encryption can be applied to data at rest, in transit, and in use.

It's a critical component of protecting data in scenarios like data breaches or theft of mobile devices.

Regularly updating and patching software and systems is a fundamental OpSec practice.

Many cyberattacks target known vulnerabilities in software and operating systems.

By keeping systems up to date, organizations reduce the likelihood of falling victim to exploits that target outdated software.

Implementing a strong password policy is another OpSec measure that's often underestimated.

Weak passwords are a common entry point for attackers.

A robust password policy encourages the use of complex, unique passwords and enforces regular password changes.

Multi-factor authentication (MFA) is also a valuable addition to password security, providing an additional layer of protection.

OpSec extends to secure communication practices.

This includes using encrypted communication channels, especially when transmitting sensitive information.

Secure email protocols and encrypted messaging apps help protect the confidentiality of communications.

Additionally, OpSec considers the risks posed by third-party vendors and partners.

When working with external entities, it's essential to evaluate their security practices and ensure they align with OpSec requirements.

Failure to do so can introduce vulnerabilities into an organization's operational environment.

It's important to remember that operational security is an ongoing process, not a one-time task.

As technology evolves and threats become more sophisticated, OpSec measures must adapt and evolve as well.

Regularly reviewing and updating OpSec practices is essential to staying ahead of potential risks.

In summary, operational security is a comprehensive approach to protecting sensitive information and assets from a wide range of threats.

It encompasses principles such as need-to-know, risk assessment, information classification, access controls, physical security, security awareness, and encryption.

By implementing these principles and best practices, organizations can significantly enhance their security posture and minimize the risk of data breaches and other security incidents.

Chapter 3: Building a Strong Security Foundation

Foundational security concepts form the bedrock of any robust cybersecurity strategy, serving as the building blocks for safeguarding digital assets and information.

These concepts are the cornerstone upon which more advanced security measures are built, making them essential for individuals and organizations alike.

One of the core concepts in cybersecurity is the principle of confidentiality, which focuses on limiting access to sensitive information only to those who are authorized to view it.

Confidentiality ensures that data remains private and protected from unauthorized access, whether it's personal, financial, or sensitive corporate information.

Integrity is another foundational concept, emphasizing the accuracy and reliability of data.

Ensuring data integrity means that information remains unaltered and trustworthy throughout its lifecycle.

Availability is equally critical, as it guarantees that data and systems are accessible when needed.

Downtime or unavailability can lead to significant disruptions and financial losses.

Authentication and authorization are fundamental principles that ensure that only authorized individuals or entities can access specific resources or information.

Authentication verifies the identity of users, while authorization determines what actions they are allowed to perform once authenticated.

Non-repudiation is a concept that prevents individuals from denying their actions or transactions.

It ensures that parties involved in a transaction cannot later deny their participation or claim that they didn't perform specific actions.

Defense in depth is a strategic security concept that involves implementing multiple layers of security measures to protect against various threats.

This approach recognizes that no single security measure is foolproof, and by layering defenses, an organization can better mitigate risks.

Vulnerabilities and threats are key components of cybersecurity understanding.

Vulnerabilities are weaknesses or flaws in systems or software that can be exploited by attackers.

Threats encompass the potential harm that can result from exploiting vulnerabilities.

Risk management is a foundational concept that involves identifying, assessing, and mitigating risks to an organization's assets and operations.

It's about making informed decisions to balance security needs with business objectives.

Firewalls are a fundamental security technology that serves as a barrier between an organization's internal network and external threats.

Firewalls filter incoming and outgoing network traffic based on a set of predefined security rules.

Encryption is a powerful concept that involves converting data into an unreadable format, making it indecipherable to unauthorized individuals or entities.

This ensures the confidentiality and security of sensitive data, even if it's intercepted.

Security policies and procedures are essential for defining and enforcing security practices within an organization.

They provide clear guidelines on how to protect information and systems, ensuring that everyone understands their roles and responsibilities.

Patch management is a critical operational concept that involves regularly updating and applying patches to software and systems.

These patches fix known vulnerabilities, reducing the risk of exploitation by attackers.

Incident response is a foundational security practice that outlines how an organization should respond to security incidents.

It includes procedures for identifying, mitigating, and recovering from security breaches.

Security awareness is an ongoing effort to educate and train individuals within an organization about security risks and best practices.

A well-informed workforce is better equipped to recognize and respond to security threats.

Physical security is a foundational concept that focuses on protecting an organization's physical assets, such as buildings, equipment, and data centers.

Measures like access controls, surveillance, and security personnel contribute to physical security.

Social engineering is a security concept that involves manipulating individuals to divulge confidential information or perform actions that compromise security.

Attackers use psychological tactics to exploit human weaknesses.

Asset management is essential for identifying and tracking an organization's assets, including hardware, software, and data.

This helps ensure that all assets are appropriately protected.

Security testing and assessments involve evaluating an organization's security measures through techniques like penetration testing, vulnerability scanning, and security audits.

These tests help identify weaknesses that need to be addressed.

Identity and access management (IAM) is a foundational concept for managing user identities and controlling their access to resources.

IAM solutions ensure that users have appropriate permissions and are authenticated securely.

Intrusion detection and prevention systems (IDS/IPS) are security technologies that monitor network traffic and identify suspicious or malicious activities.

They can either detect and alert or actively block such activities.

Security incident and event management (SIEM) systems are used to collect, analyze, and correlate security event data from various sources.

They provide insights into security incidents and trends.

Compliance is a foundational concept that involves adhering to laws, regulations, and industry standards related to cybersecurity.

It ensures that an organization meets legal and regulatory requirements.

Network segmentation is a security strategy that divides a network into smaller segments, limiting the lateral movement of attackers within the network.

This containment helps prevent the spread of threats.

Security updates and patches are essential for keeping software, operating systems, and devices secure.

Vendors release updates to fix vulnerabilities and improve security.

User awareness and training programs are instrumental in ensuring that individuals understand the importance of security and how to protect sensitive information.

Regular training helps create a security-conscious culture.

Cloud security is a foundational concept that addresses the unique security challenges of cloud computing.

It involves securing data, applications, and services in cloud environments.

Security monitoring and incident response capabilities are critical for detecting and responding to security threats promptly.

Continuous monitoring helps identify and mitigate security incidents in real-time.

These foundational security concepts provide a solid framework for individuals and organizations to build effective cybersecurity strategies.

By understanding and implementing these principles, you can better protect your digital assets and information from a wide range of threats.

Security frameworks and models play a vital role in the field of cybersecurity, providing structured approaches to assess, plan, and implement security measures.

These frameworks and models serve as essential guides for individuals and organizations seeking to strengthen their security posture.

One widely recognized security framework is the NIST Cybersecurity Framework, developed by the National Institute of Standards and Technology (NIST).

This framework outlines a set of guidelines and best practices for managing and reducing cybersecurity risk.

The NIST Cybersecurity Framework is based on five core functions: Identify, Protect, Detect, Respond, and Recover.

Identify involves understanding and managing cybersecurity risks, including asset management and risk assessment.

Protect focuses on implementing safeguards and security measures to mitigate identified risks.

Detect emphasizes continuous monitoring and the early detection of security incidents.

Respond involves taking prompt and effective action when a security incident occurs.

Recover focuses on restoring services and systems to normal operation after an incident.

Another well-known framework is the ISO 27001, which sets the international standard for information security management systems (ISMS).

ISO 27001 provides a systematic and risk-based approach to managing information security.

It includes processes for risk assessment, security policy development, and continuous improvement.

The CIS (Center for Internet Security) Controls provide a prioritized set of actions for organizations to improve their cybersecurity posture.

These controls cover a wide range of security areas, from inventory and control of hardware assets to secure configuration and data protection.

The CIS Controls are organized into three implementation groups, making them adaptable to different organizational sizes and needs.

The Zero Trust security model is gaining popularity as organizations shift away from the traditional perimeter-based approach to security.

Zero Trust assumes that threats can exist both inside and outside the network and requires verification and strict access controls for all users and devices.

The model's core principles include "verify explicitly" and "least privilege access."

The Defense in Depth security strategy is another widely used concept, emphasizing multiple layers of security controls to protect against various threats.

By layering defenses, organizations can reduce the risk of a single point of failure and increase overall security.

Security frameworks and models provide organizations with structured approaches to assess and improve their cybersecurity posture.

They offer valuable guidance on identifying risks, implementing protective measures, detecting security incidents, responding to breaches, and recovering from them.

Adopting these frameworks and models can help organizations establish a proactive and comprehensive security strategy.

One of the essential components of security frameworks and models is risk assessment.

Risk assessment involves identifying, analyzing, and prioritizing potential risks to an organization's assets and operations.

By understanding these risks, organizations can make informed decisions about where to allocate resources for security improvements.

Security frameworks and models often provide templates and guidelines for conducting risk assessments.

The choice of a specific framework or model depends on an organization's industry, regulatory requirements, and unique security needs.

Some organizations may opt to use a combination of frameworks and models to create a tailored security strategy.

For example, an organization operating in the healthcare sector may need to comply with the Health Insurance Portability and Accountability Act (HIPAA) regulations.

In this case, they might choose to use the NIST Cybersecurity Framework as a foundation and integrate specific HIPAA requirements into their security program.

Frameworks and models also play a crucial role in compliance management.

Many regulatory authorities and industry standards bodies reference established frameworks and models in their guidelines.

Organizations can use these frameworks as a roadmap to align their security practices with regulatory requirements.

The adoption of security frameworks and models is not limited to large enterprises.

Small and medium-sized businesses can also benefit from these structured approaches to cybersecurity.

In fact, frameworks like the CIS Controls offer adaptable security strategies suitable for organizations of all sizes.

When implementing a security framework or model, organizations should consider the following key steps:

Assessment: Begin by assessing the organization's current security posture. Identify strengths, weaknesses, and areas for improvement.

Objective Setting: Establish clear security objectives and goals. What are you trying to achieve with your security program?

Framework Selection: Choose the appropriate framework or model that aligns with your organization's needs and industry requirements.

Customization: Tailor the framework or model to fit your organization's specific circumstances. Not all components may be relevant, so focus on what matters most.

Implementation: Implement the security controls and measures outlined in the framework or model. This may involve changes to policies, procedures, and technical configurations.

Monitoring: Continuously monitor your security environment for threats and vulnerabilities. Regularly review and update your security measures to adapt to changing risks.

Assessment: Periodically assess the effectiveness of your security program. Conduct security audits and assessments to ensure compliance and identify areas for improvement.

Documentation: Maintain clear documentation of your security policies, procedures, and incidents. Documentation is essential for compliance and incident response.

Training and Awareness: Educate your staff and stakeholders about security best practices and their roles in maintaining a secure environment.

Incident Response: Develop a comprehensive incident response plan that outlines how to respond to security incidents effectively.

Security frameworks and models are valuable tools for organizations seeking to enhance their cybersecurity posture and protect sensitive information.

By following the principles and guidelines provided by these frameworks, organizations can establish a strong foundation for security, reduce risks, and respond effectively to security incidents when they occur.

Ultimately, the adoption of security frameworks and models contributes to a safer digital landscape for individuals, businesses, and society as a whole.

Chapter 4: Network Security Fundamentals

Network threats and vulnerabilities are ever-present challenges in the realm of cybersecurity, posing risks to individuals, organizations, and even nations.

Understanding these threats and vulnerabilities is essential for building a robust defense and safeguarding the integrity and confidentiality of digital information.

One of the most common network threats is malware, malicious software designed to infiltrate, disrupt, or steal data from target systems.

Viruses, for instance, are programs that attach themselves to legitimate files and replicate when those files are executed.

Worms, on the other hand, don't require a host file and can propagate independently across networks, often with the goal of compromising vulnerable systems.

Trojans, aptly named after the legendary wooden horse, disguise themselves as legitimate programs to deceive users into downloading and executing them, enabling unauthorized access or data theft.

Ransomware, a particularly disruptive threat, encrypts victims' files and demands a ransom for decryption keys, often causing financial losses and data breaches.

Phishing is another prevalent network threat where cybercriminals craft convincing emails or messages to trick recipients into revealing sensitive information like login credentials or financial details.

Spear phishing takes this a step further by customizing the attack for specific individuals or organizations, making it even more challenging to detect.

Social engineering attacks manipulate human psychology, often exploiting trust or urgency to trick victims into divulging information or performing actions they wouldn't otherwise do.

Distributed Denial of Service (DDoS) attacks flood a target's network or website with a massive volume of traffic, overwhelming it and rendering it inaccessible to users.

IoT devices, with their often lax security measures, have become attractive targets for attackers to compromise and use in DDoS attacks.

Zero-day vulnerabilities are software flaws unknown to the vendor, making them prime targets for exploitation.

Attackers who discover or purchase such vulnerabilities can develop exploits to breach systems before patches are available.

Advanced Persistent Threats (APTs) are highly sophisticated and targeted attacks, often associated with nation-states or well-funded cybercriminal groups.

These attackers operate quietly, infiltrating systems and maintaining access for extended periods, enabling data theft or espionage.

Brute force attacks involve systematically trying all possible combinations of passwords or encryption keys until the correct one is found.

Weak or easily guessable passwords are particularly vulnerable to this type of attack.

Man-in-the-Middle (MitM) attacks intercept communication between two parties, allowing the attacker to eavesdrop, modify, or inject malicious content.

Pharming attacks redirect website traffic to fraudulent sites without the user's knowledge, often used for phishing purposes.

Drive-by downloads occur when a user visits a compromised website that automatically initiates the download of malicious software to their device.

Cross-Site Scripting (XSS) attacks inject malicious scripts into web pages viewed by other users, potentially leading to the theft of their data or session cookies.

SQL injection attacks manipulate web application databases by inserting malicious SQL code into user inputs, potentially exposing sensitive data or compromising the application itself.

Watering hole attacks involve compromising websites that are likely to be visited by the target audience, such as employees of a specific company or members of an industry group.

Fileless malware operates in memory, leaving no trace on disk, making it challenging to detect and eradicate.

Cryptojacking is the unauthorized use of a victim's computing resources to mine cryptocurrency, slowing down the device and increasing energy costs.

Malvertising spreads malware through online ads, often on legitimate websites, exploiting vulnerabilities in the ad platform or user's browser.

Whaling attacks target high-profile individuals within organizations, such as CEOs or executives, with the goal of stealing sensitive information or financial assets.

Understanding these network threats is crucial, but it's equally important to be aware of network vulnerabilities that can be exploited by attackers.

Software vulnerabilities are weaknesses in software code that can be exploited to compromise a system or application.

These vulnerabilities can range from programming errors to design flaws, and they are often patched by software vendors when discovered.

However, organizations must regularly update and patch their software to mitigate these vulnerabilities effectively.

Operating system vulnerabilities are particularly attractive to attackers because they can provide a foothold into a system. By exploiting vulnerabilities in the underlying operating system, attackers can gain access to sensitive data and compromise the entire network.

Hardware vulnerabilities, although less common, can have significant consequences.

Flaws in hardware components or firmware can create backdoors or allow unauthorized access to devices.

Network configuration errors are a common source of vulnerabilities.

Misconfigured firewalls, routers, and other network devices can inadvertently expose sensitive data or provide unauthorized access points.

Weak or default passwords are a well-known vulnerability that attackers often exploit.

Organizations should enforce strong password policies and encourage the use of multi-factor authentication (MFA) to enhance security.

Outdated or unpatched software and systems are a prime target for attackers.

Vulnerabilities that have known patches but haven't been addressed present a significant risk.

Third-party software and plugins can introduce vulnerabilities into an organization's network.

These components should be carefully vetted and kept up to date.

Social engineering attacks prey on human psychology and can exploit vulnerabilities in individuals.

Training and awareness programs can help employees recognize and resist these attacks.

Network threats and vulnerabilities are dynamic, evolving over time as technology advances and attackers become more sophisticated.

To effectively defend against these threats, organizations must adopt a proactive and multi-layered approach to cybersecurity.

This includes regularly updating and patching systems, implementing strong access controls, and providing ongoing security training for staff.

Additionally, organizations should stay informed about emerging threats and adapt their security strategies accordingly.

By understanding both the nature of network threats and the vulnerabilities that can be exploited, individuals and organizations can better protect themselves in an increasingly interconnected and digital world.

Network security controls and technologies form the front line of defense against a multitude of cyber threats, safeguarding the integrity, confidentiality, and availability of digital assets.

These essential measures and tools work collectively to fortify networks and protect against malicious actors seeking to exploit vulnerabilities.

Firewalls, often considered the guardians of the network, act as barriers that scrutinize incoming and outgoing traffic.

They apply predefined rules to determine whether data packets should be allowed or blocked based on factors like source, destination, and content.

Intrusion Detection Systems (IDS) and Intrusion Prevention Systems (IPS) play pivotal roles in identifying and thwarting suspicious activities.

IDS passively monitor network traffic, while IPS actively intervene to block potentially harmful traffic based on predefined signatures or behavioral anomalies.

Virtual Private Networks (VPNs) create secure tunnels over public networks, encrypting data to ensure confidentiality and secure remote access.

Access Control Lists (ACLs) provide granular control over who can access specific resources, regulating network traffic at the port or protocol level.

Network Segmentation divides networks into smaller, isolated segments, limiting the lateral movement of threats and reducing the attack surface.

Proxy servers act as intermediaries between users and the internet, enhancing security by filtering requests and hiding internal network details.

Intrusion Detection and Prevention Systems (IDPS) go beyond monitoring and prevention, offering advanced capabilities like behavioral analysis and anomaly detection.

Load Balancers distribute incoming network traffic evenly across multiple servers, optimizing performance and ensuring high availability.

Network-based Antivirus and Anti-malware solutions scan network traffic for known malware signatures and suspicious behavior.

Content Filtering solutions block access to specific websites or content categories, preventing users from accessing potentially harmful or unproductive sites.

Email Security Gateways filter incoming and outgoing email traffic to detect and block spam, phishing attempts, and malicious attachments.

Web Application Firewalls (WAFs) protect web applications by filtering and monitoring incoming traffic, mitigating attacks like SQL injection and cross-site scripting.

Next-Generation Firewalls (NGFWs) combine traditional firewall capabilities with advanced features like application-level filtering and threat intelligence integration.

Network Access Control (NAC) systems ensure that only compliant and authorized devices gain network access, enhancing security and compliance.

Network Security Monitoring (NSM) tools provide real-time visibility into network activities, enabling early detection of threats and rapid response.

Security Information and Event Management (SIEM) platforms collect and analyze security data from various sources, offering insights into network security incidents.

Secure Sockets Layer (SSL) and Transport Layer Security (TLS) protocols encrypt data transmitted over the internet, protecting against eavesdropping and data tampering.

Secure Shell (SSH) is a cryptographic protocol used for secure remote access and file transfers, replacing insecure protocols like Telnet.

Network security controls and technologies are essential components of a comprehensive cybersecurity strategy.

They serve as the foundation for securing digital assets, ensuring data protection, and safeguarding network infrastructure.

Firewalls, the cornerstone of network security, stand as the first line of defense, diligently examining traffic to permit or block it according to predefined rules.

Intrusion Detection Systems (IDS) and Intrusion Prevention Systems (IPS) bolster this defense, offering continuous monitoring and automated threat response.

Virtual Private Networks (VPNs) create secure channels over the internet, protecting data from eavesdropping while enabling secure remote access.

Access Control Lists (ACLs) provide fine-grained control over network resources, dictating who can access specific assets and under what conditions.

Network Segmentation isolates segments of the network, curtailing lateral movement and reducing exposure to threats.

Proxy servers enhance security by serving as intermediaries, filtering requests and obfuscating internal network details.

Intrusion Detection and Prevention Systems (IDPS) offer advanced capabilities, such as behavior analysis, anomaly detection, and threat intelligence integration.

Load Balancers optimize network performance and ensure high availability by distributing incoming traffic evenly across multiple servers.

Network-based Antivirus and Anti-malware solutions scan network traffic for known malware signatures and signs of malicious activity.

Content Filtering solutions restrict access to specific websites or content categories, reducing the risk of exposure to harmful or unproductive content.

Email Security Gateways filter email traffic, blocking spam, phishing attempts, and malicious attachments to safeguard email communication.

Web Application Firewalls (WAFs) protect web applications by monitoring and filtering incoming traffic, shielding against threats like SQL injection and cross-site scripting.

Next-Generation Firewalls (NGFWs) combine traditional firewall capabilities with advanced features like application-level filtering and integration with threat intelligence feeds.

Network Access Control (NAC) systems ensure that only compliant and authorized devices gain network access, enforcing security and compliance policies.

Network Security Monitoring (NSM) tools offer real-time visibility into network activities, empowering early threat detection and swift response.

Security Information and Event Management (SIEM) platforms collect and analyze security data from diverse sources, providing valuable insights into security incidents.

Secure Sockets Layer (SSL) and Transport Layer Security (TLS) protocols encrypt data transmitted over the internet, safeguarding against interception and tampering.

Secure Shell (SSH) protocols secure remote access and file transfers, replacing insecure alternatives like Telnet.

These network security controls and technologies work harmoniously, creating layers of defense that shield against a multitude of threats.

The synergy between firewalls, IDS/IPS, VPNs, and access controls ensures that only authorized entities traverse the network while malicious activities are swiftly intercepted and halted.

Content filtering, email security, and web application firewalls add additional layers of protection by scrutinizing data and communication channels.

Load balancers enhance efficiency, reducing downtime and ensuring uninterrupted service.

IDPS systems employ behavioral analysis and anomaly detection to identify elusive threats, working in tandem with SIEM platforms to provide real-time threat intelligence.

Network segmentation, NAC, and SSH protocols contribute to a robust security posture, controlling access and securing remote connections.

In this interconnected world, the importance of network security controls and technologies cannot be overstated.

They serve as the bedrock of cybersecurity, fortifying networks against an array of threats and vulnerabilities.

A well-constructed network security strategy combines these measures and technologies to create a resilient defense, enabling individuals and organizations to navigate the digital landscape with confidence.

By understanding the roles and capabilities of these components, individuals and organizations can better protect their assets, preserve their privacy, and ensure the integrity of their networked systems.

Chapter 5: Endpoint Protection and Device Security

Endpoint security, the practice of safeguarding individual devices, such as computers, laptops, smartphones, and tablets, is a critical aspect of a comprehensive cybersecurity strategy.

In an increasingly connected world, where the boundaries between personal and professional use of devices blur, securing these endpoints is of paramount importance.

One of the foundational best practices in endpoint security is ensuring that all devices are equipped with up-to-date antivirus and anti-malware software.

These programs protect against known threats and provide an additional layer of defense against malicious software.

Regular software updates and patches are essential, as they address vulnerabilities that attackers often exploit.

Keeping operating systems, applications, and firmware current is crucial to reducing the attack surface.

Implementing a robust access control policy helps restrict who can access devices and what they can do once they gain access.

Role-based access control (RBAC) and least privilege principle ensure that users have the minimum permissions necessary to perform their tasks, reducing the risk of privilege escalation attacks.

Device encryption is a fundamental practice to protect data stored on endpoints.

Full-disk encryption and encryption of sensitive files ensure that even if a device is lost or stolen, the data remains confidential.

Multi-factor authentication (MFA) is an effective way to verify the identity of users trying to access devices and data.

By requiring multiple forms of authentication, such as a password and a biometric scan, MFA adds an extra layer of security.

Endpoint detection and response (EDR) solutions provide real-time monitoring and threat detection capabilities.

They can identify suspicious activities and respond automatically to mitigate threats.

Implementing strong and unique passwords for each device is crucial, as weak or reused passwords are a common entry point for attackers.

Password management tools can help users generate, store, and retrieve complex passwords securely.

Regularly backing up data on endpoints ensures that critical information can be restored in the event of a ransomware attack, hardware failure, or data loss incident.

Backup processes should be automated and include off-site or cloud storage for redundancy.

Intrusion detection and prevention systems (IDS/IPS) can monitor endpoint traffic for suspicious patterns or known attack signatures.

They can block malicious activities or generate alerts for further investigation.

Remote device management capabilities allow organizations to enforce security policies, update software, and monitor endpoints remotely.

This is particularly important for organizations with a distributed workforce or a large number of devices.

Educating end-users about cybersecurity risks and best practices is a vital aspect of endpoint security.

Regular training and awareness programs can help users recognize phishing attempts, social engineering tactics, and other threats.

Implementing a robust incident response plan is essential.

In the event of a security incident, a well-defined plan outlines the steps to take, ensuring a swift and effective response.

Mobile device management (MDM) solutions are crucial for securing smartphones and tablets used in business settings.

MDM allows organizations to enforce security policies, remotely wipe devices, and control access to corporate resources.

Implementing application whitelisting, which allows only approved applications to run on endpoints, can prevent unauthorized or malicious software from executing.

Behavioral analysis and anomaly detection tools can identify unusual activities on endpoints, helping to detect previously unknown threats.

Network segmentation can limit the lateral movement of threats within a network, reducing the potential impact of a compromised endpoint.

Implementing data loss prevention (DLP) solutions can help prevent sensitive data from being leaked or shared inappropriately.

DLP tools can monitor and control the movement of sensitive data on endpoints and across the network.

Regularly conducting vulnerability assessments and penetration testing on endpoints can help identify weaknesses that need to be addressed.

These assessments should be followed by prompt remediation of any identified vulnerabilities.

Endpoint security should extend to removable media, such as USB drives, which can introduce malware or compromise endpoints when connected.

Endpoint security solutions should include controls for scanning and monitoring removable media.

Implementing secure boot processes and secure boot chains can help ensure that the device's firmware and operating system are not tampered with during startup.

Privileged access management (PAM) solutions can help organizations manage and monitor privileged accounts and access on endpoints, reducing the risk of insider threats.

File integrity monitoring (FIM) solutions can detect unauthorized changes to critical system files and configurations.

They can provide early warning of potential compromises.

Containerization and application sandboxing can isolate applications and their data from the underlying operating system, adding a layer of security.

Regularly auditing and monitoring endpoint activities can help detect and respond to security incidents promptly.

Logging and monitoring solutions should be configured to capture relevant security events.

Implementing a robust patch management process is essential to keep endpoints protected against known vulnerabilities.

This process should be systematic and prioritize critical patches.

Using advanced threat intelligence feeds and threat hunting techniques can help proactively identify and mitigate threats on endpoints.

Machine learning and artificial intelligence technologies can enhance endpoint security by identifying patterns and anomalies associated with malicious activities.

Security information and event management (SIEM) solutions can aggregate and correlate endpoint logs and events, providing a comprehensive view of the security posture.

Implementing endpoint security best practices is an ongoing effort that requires vigilance and adaptability.

Cyber threats evolve continuously, and organizations must stay ahead by updating their security measures and practices.

By adopting a holistic approach to endpoint security, organizations can better protect their devices, data, and networks, reducing the risk of security breaches and data loss.

Educating users, leveraging technology, and maintaining a proactive stance are key to ensuring the security of endpoints in an ever-changing threat landscape.

Device security configuration and management are crucial aspects of maintaining a robust cybersecurity posture in today's digital landscape.

Devices, including computers, mobile phones, tablets, and IoT (Internet of Things) devices, are integral to our daily lives and business operations.

However, they also represent significant targets for cyber threats, making it imperative to establish effective security practices.

One fundamental principle of device security is ensuring that devices are configured securely from the outset.

This includes installing the latest operating system updates and security patches, as vulnerabilities in the system can be exploited by attackers.

Device manufacturers frequently release updates to address known security issues, and keeping devices up to date is an essential step in reducing the risk of exploitation.

Moreover, it is essential to configure and enforce strong password policies for devices.

Weak or easily guessable passwords are a common entry point for attackers.

Implementing complex password requirements and encouraging the use of passphrases can significantly enhance security.

Multi-factor authentication (MFA) is another critical aspect of device security.

MFA adds an extra layer of protection by requiring users to provide multiple forms of authentication, such as a password and a one-time code sent to their mobile device, before gaining access.

This additional layer of security can thwart unauthorized access attempts, even if a password is compromised.

Device encryption is a key measure to protect data at rest.

Encrypting the device's storage ensures that even if it is lost or stolen, the data remains unreadable without the proper decryption key.

Both full-disk encryption and file-level encryption should be considered based on the sensitivity of the data.

Managing and controlling user access to devices is essential.

Implementing role-based access control (RBAC) ensures that users have the minimum necessary permissions to perform their tasks.

This practice limits the potential damage an attacker can do if they gain access to a device.

Regularly auditing user accounts and access permissions helps maintain security and compliance.

Network connectivity and communication settings on devices should be carefully configured.

For example, disabling unnecessary network services and ports reduces the attack surface and minimizes the risk of exploitation.

Firewalls, both at the device and network levels, play a vital role in protecting devices from unauthorized network traffic and external threats.

It is crucial to configure and monitor firewall rules to ensure that only legitimate traffic is allowed.

Mobile device management (MDM) solutions are essential for securing smartphones and tablets in enterprise environments.

MDM allows organizations to enforce security policies, remotely wipe devices in case of loss or theft, and control access to corporate resources.

Managing software applications and updates on devices is critical.

Implementing application whitelisting, which allows only approved applications to run, can prevent unauthorized or malicious software from executing.

Moreover, regularly updating software and applications is essential for patching known vulnerabilities.

Regularly auditing devices for software vulnerabilities is crucial.

Vulnerability assessments and penetration testing help identify weaknesses that need to be addressed.

This should be followed by prompt remediation of any identified vulnerabilities to reduce the risk of exploitation. Endpoint detection and response (EDR) solutions provide real-time monitoring and threat detection capabilities.

Chapter 6: Access Control and Identity Management

Access control is a fundamental concept in the realm of cybersecurity, governing who is allowed to access what resources in a computing environment.

It serves as a critical component of information security, ensuring that sensitive data and systems are protected from unauthorized access and potential breaches.

Access control models and principles provide the framework for designing and implementing effective access control systems.

One of the fundamental principles of access control is the principle of least privilege (PoLP).

This principle dictates that users should only be granted the minimum level of access or permissions required to perform their job functions.

By limiting unnecessary privileges, organizations reduce the risk of unauthorized access and potential misuse of resources.

Role-based access control (RBAC) is a widely used access control model that aligns with the principle of least privilege.

In RBAC, access is granted based on an individual's role or job function within an organization.

This approach simplifies access management by categorizing users into roles with predefined sets of permissions.

Another access control model is discretionary access control (DAC), where resource owners have control over who can access their resources.

In DAC, resource owners can grant or revoke access to their resources as they see fit, providing a high degree of flexibility but potentially leading to inconsistent access control.

Mandatory access control (MAC) is a stricter access control model commonly used in government and military environments.

In MAC, access decisions are based on security labels and rules defined by a central authority.

Subjects (users or processes) and objects (resources) are assigned labels, and access is determined by comparing labels and rules.

Attribute-based access control (ABAC) is a more dynamic access control model that considers a variety of attributes, such as user attributes, resource attributes, and environmental attributes, in access decisions.

ABAC allows for fine-grained control based on contextual information.

Access control lists (ACLs) and capability lists are mechanisms used to implement access control in various models.

ACLs specify who can access a resource and what actions they can perform, while capability lists provide users with tokens that grant access to specific resources.

Authentication is a critical component of access control, ensuring that individuals or entities are who they claim to be.

Common authentication methods include passwords, biometrics, smart cards, and multi-factor authentication (MFA).

Authorization is the process of determining what actions an authenticated user or entity is allowed to perform.

It is closely related to access control, as authorization decisions are based on the permissions associated with a user or role.

Audit trails and logging are essential for monitoring and maintaining access control.

They record access attempts, successful or unsuccessful, providing an audit trail that can be used for security analysis and compliance.

Access control principles emphasize the importance of separation of duties, where no single individual should have complete control over a critical process or resource.

This helps prevent fraud, errors, and misuse of power.

The principle of accountability underscores the need to trace actions back to the responsible individual or entity, ensuring that there are consequences for unauthorized access or actions.

In practice, access control models and principles are implemented through various technologies and mechanisms.

Access control lists (ACLs) are commonly used to specify who can access a resource and what actions they can perform.

For example, a file system ACL might specify that User A has read and write access to a specific file, while User B has only read access.

Role-based access control (RBAC) is widely used in organizations to manage access to systems and resources.

In RBAC, users are assigned roles, and roles are associated with specific permissions.

For instance, an organization might have an "HR Manager" role that grants access to HR-related systems and data.

Attribute-based access control (ABAC) takes a more flexible approach, considering a wide range of attributes in access decisions.

For example, ABAC can take into account a user's location, time of access, and other contextual information when determining access rights.

Authentication mechanisms, such as biometrics or smart cards, play a crucial role in verifying the identity of users or entities.

Multi-factor authentication (MFA) combines multiple authentication methods, adding an extra layer of security.

Authorization systems enforce access control policies by determining whether a user or entity has the necessary permissions to perform a specific action.

This is often based on the user's authenticated identity and associated attributes.

Logging and monitoring mechanisms record access attempts and actions taken, creating an audit trail that can be reviewed for security analysis and compliance purposes.

Access control models and principles are foundational to cybersecurity, ensuring that only authorized individuals or entities can access resources and perform actions within an organization's computing environment.

By implementing effective access control mechanisms and adhering to access control principles, organizations can significantly enhance their security posture and protect against unauthorized access and data breaches.

Identity and Access Management (IAM) solutions are a cornerstone of modern cybersecurity, playing a pivotal role in safeguarding digital resources and ensuring that only authorized users gain access to sensitive information and systems.

IAM encompasses a set of technologies, policies, and processes designed to manage digital identities, control access to resources, and enforce security policies.

At its core, IAM revolves around the management of user identities, including employees, contractors, partners, and customers, as well as the resources they need to access.

Central to IAM is the concept of authentication, which verifies the identity of users before granting access.

Authentication methods range from traditional usernames and passwords to more advanced techniques like biometrics, smart cards, and multi-factor authentication (MFA).

MFA, in particular, has gained prominence as it requires users to provide two or more factors of authentication, adding an extra layer of security.

Once a user's identity is authenticated, IAM solutions enforce access control policies based on predefined rules and permissions.

These policies dictate who can access what resources and what actions they are allowed to perform.

Role-based access control (RBAC) and attribute-based access control (ABAC) are commonly used models for defining access control policies.

RBAC assigns users to roles, with each role having a specific set of permissions.

ABAC, on the other hand, considers a wide range of attributes, such as user attributes, resource attributes, and contextual information, when making access decisions.

IAM solutions also provide tools for user provisioning and de-provisioning, ensuring that users receive the appropriate access when they join an organization and that access is promptly revoked when they leave.

Automated provisioning helps streamline administrative tasks and reduce the risk of unauthorized access.

Furthermore, IAM solutions offer Single Sign-On (SSO) capabilities, allowing users to access multiple applications and services with a single set of credentials.

SSO not only enhances user convenience but also simplifies access management and reduces the risk of password-related security incidents.

IAM solutions are not limited to managing human identities; they also extend to managing non-human identities, such as service accounts, applications, and devices.

These non-human identities play a crucial role in modern IT ecosystems, and IAM solutions help ensure their secure management and authentication.

Privileged Access Management (PAM) is a specialized subset of IAM that focuses on managing and monitoring privileged accounts and access.

Privileged accounts, such as administrative and root accounts, have elevated permissions and can pose significant security risks if not properly controlled.

PAM solutions enforce strict access controls, session recording, and monitoring of privileged access to mitigate these risks.

IAM solutions are also vital for ensuring compliance with industry regulations and data protection laws.

They provide audit trails, logs, and reporting capabilities that help organizations demonstrate adherence to security and privacy requirements.

As businesses increasingly adopt cloud computing and hybrid IT environments, IAM solutions have evolved to address the unique challenges of these environments.

Cloud Identity and Access Management (CIAM) solutions are tailored to manage identities and access in the cloud, providing secure authentication and authorization for cloud-based applications and services.

API Gateways and Identity as a Service (IDaaS) offerings are integral components of CIAM, helping organizations secure interactions between users and cloud-based resources.

IAM solutions play a crucial role in enhancing security while enabling digital transformation and remote workforces.

By implementing IAM best practices, organizations can ensure that their employees, partners, and customers can access the right resources at the right time while minimizing security risks.

However, IAM implementation is not without challenges.

Managing a growing number of identities, ensuring seamless integration with various applications, and keeping up with evolving threats require careful planning and continuous monitoring.

Additionally, user experience and ease of use are essential aspects of IAM, as overly complex authentication processes can lead to user frustration and security shortcuts.

In summary, Identity and Access Management solutions are central to modern cybersecurity strategies, enabling organizations to manage identities, control access, and enforce security policies.

IAM enhances security by verifying user identities and ensuring that only authorized individuals or entities can access digital resources.

It simplifies access management, improves compliance, and plays a pivotal role in securing cloud and hybrid environments.

As the digital landscape continues to evolve, IAM solutions will remain a critical component of cybersecurity, helping organizations adapt to changing threats and business requirements while safeguarding their digital assets.

Chapter 7: Incident Response Basics

Incident identification and classification are essential components of incident management, forming the foundation for an effective response to cybersecurity incidents.

In the ever-evolving landscape of cyber threats, organizations must be prepared to swiftly identify and categorize incidents to minimize damage and protect their assets.

At its core, incident identification involves recognizing that an incident has occurred within an organization's IT environment.

This initial step often relies on various detection mechanisms, including intrusion detection systems, antivirus software, security information and event management (SIEM) tools, and user reports.

Detection mechanisms continuously monitor network traffic, system logs, and behavior patterns to identify deviations or suspicious activities that may indicate an incident.

User reports are valuable sources of information, as employees or system users may notice unusual behavior or signs of compromise.

Once an incident is detected, the next crucial step is classification, where the incident is categorized based on its nature, severity, and impact.

Classification is a critical task that helps organizations prioritize their response efforts appropriately.

Common classifications include security incidents, data breaches, malware infections, denial-of-service attacks, and unauthorized access, among others.

Each classification may have its response playbook and requires specific actions to mitigate the incident effectively.

Incident classification often depends on the organization's established incident response policies and procedures.

Security incidents, for example, involve events that indicate a potential security threat, such as multiple failed login attempts or suspicious network traffic.

Data breaches, on the other hand, involve unauthorized access to sensitive data, and they are typically categorized based on the extent of the breach and the data compromised.

Malware infections encompass incidents where malicious software has infiltrated an organization's systems, and classification may involve identifying the type and severity of the malware.

Denial-of-service (DoS) attacks involve incidents where attackers attempt to overwhelm a system or network with traffic, rendering it unavailable to users.

Unauthorized access incidents involve unauthorized individuals gaining access to systems or resources, often through exploiting vulnerabilities or weak credentials.

The classification process also considers the potential impact of the incident.

Incident responders assess the severity of the incident based on factors like the number of systems affected, the sensitivity of the data exposed, and the potential business impact.

This assessment helps determine the appropriate level of response and resource allocation.

For example, a minor security incident with limited impact may require a less intensive response effort compared to a major data breach that exposes sensitive customer information.

Additionally, organizations often classify incidents based on the attackers' motivations and the methods used.

These classifications can include cyber espionage, financial fraud, hacktivism, and insider threats.

Understanding the motivation behind an incident can provide valuable insights into the attackers' goals and tactics, aiding in the development of effective response strategies.

Incident identification and classification are iterative processes that require collaboration between IT security teams, incident responders, and relevant stakeholders.

Organizations should establish clear incident identification and classification procedures as part of their incident response plans.

These procedures should define roles and responsibilities, the criteria for incident classification, and the escalation process.

The incident response team should regularly train and test their incident identification and classification skills through tabletop exercises and simulations.

Furthermore, organizations should leverage technology solutions, such as SIEM systems and advanced threat detection tools, to enhance their incident identification capabilities.

Machine learning and artificial intelligence can assist in identifying patterns and anomalies that may indicate incidents, helping organizations detect and classify incidents more effectively.

Effective incident identification and classification are crucial for minimizing the impact of cybersecurity incidents.

By promptly recognizing incidents and accurately categorizing them, organizations can respond swiftly and mitigate the potential damage to their systems, data, and reputation.

Moreover, a well-established incident identification and classification process strengthens an organization's overall cybersecurity posture by facilitating continuous improvement and learning from past incidents.

In summary, incident identification and classification are fundamental steps in the incident response process.

These steps enable organizations to recognize and categorize cybersecurity incidents, guiding their response efforts to minimize damage and protect their assets.

Clear incident identification and classification procedures, along with technology solutions and training, are essential for effective incident response and overall cybersecurity resilience.

In the realm of cybersecurity, incident response teams play a pivotal role in safeguarding organizations from cyber threats and minimizing the impact of security incidents.

These teams are composed of individuals with specific roles and responsibilities, working together to detect, investigate, mitigate, and recover from security incidents effectively.

One of the key roles within an incident response team is that of the Incident Commander.

The Incident Commander is responsible for overall coordination and decision-making during an incident.

This role requires a clear understanding of the organization's incident response plan and the ability to make critical decisions swiftly.

The Incident Commander also serves as the primary point of communication with senior management and external stakeholders.

Another crucial role is that of the Incident Responder, often referred to as the "first responder."

Incident Responders are the individuals who initially identify and assess potential security incidents.

They have a deep understanding of security protocols and procedures and are trained to respond rapidly to incidents.

Their responsibilities include confirming the incident, preserving evidence, and containing the threat when possible.

Next is the Forensic Analyst, who specializes in gathering and analyzing digital evidence related to the incident.

Forensic Analysts use various tools and techniques to examine compromised systems, logs, and data to determine the extent of the breach and the methods used by the attackers.

Their findings are crucial for understanding the incident's scope and for legal and compliance purposes.

The Malware Analyst focuses specifically on analyzing and dissecting malicious software.

This role is essential in incidents involving malware infections, as Malware Analysts work to identify the type of malware, its capabilities, and potential damage.

Their analysis informs the response strategy, including malware removal and recovery efforts.

A critical function within the incident response team is that of the Network Analyst.

Network Analysts specialize in examining network traffic and logs to identify anomalous patterns and potential security threats.

Their role is to trace the attacker's movements within the network and determine the extent of the compromise.

Additionally, they assist in containing the incident by isolating affected systems or segments of the network.

The role of the Threat Intelligence Analyst involves staying informed about the latest threat landscape and providing real-time threat intelligence to the incident response team.

They analyze threat data, including indicators of compromise (IOCs) and tactics, techniques, and procedures (TTPs) used by threat actors.

Their insights help responders adapt their strategies to combat evolving threats effectively.

Legal and Compliance Advisors are integral to the incident response process, particularly in incidents that may have legal or regulatory implications.

They ensure that the response actions comply with applicable laws and regulations and assist in documenting the incident for potential legal proceedings.

The Public Relations and Communications Specialist manages external and internal communications during an incident.

This role is essential for maintaining transparency and managing the organization's reputation.

Effective communication helps reassure stakeholders, customers, and employees, reducing the impact of the incident.

The Human Resources Coordinator plays a crucial role in incidents involving personnel or insider threats.

They collaborate with legal and compliance teams to ensure that human resources policies are followed and may assist in conducting employee interviews.

The Executive Sponsor, typically a senior leader within the organization, provides guidance and support to the incident response team.

They make critical decisions regarding resource allocation and response priorities.

Additionally, the Executive Sponsor acts as a liaison between the incident response team and the executive leadership.

The Incident Recorder is responsible for documenting all incident-related activities, decisions, and actions taken during the response.

Accurate documentation is essential for post-incident analysis, reporting, and compliance purposes.

The Vendor and Third-Party Liaison may be required in incidents involving third-party vendors or service providers.

Their role is to coordinate with external entities, such as cloud service providers or cybersecurity vendors, to assist in the response efforts.

Lastly, the Recovery and Remediation Specialist focuses on restoring affected systems and services to their normal operation.

They work closely with IT teams to ensure that vulnerabilities are patched, and security controls are enhanced to prevent future incidents.

In summary, incident response teams are comprised of individuals with specific roles and responsibilities, each contributing to the efficient detection, analysis, and mitigation of security incidents.

These teams require clear communication, well-defined processes, and continuous training to effectively respond to the ever-evolving landscape of cyber threats.

Collaboration and coordination among team members are essential to minimize the impact of security incidents and protect the organization's assets and reputation.

Chapter 8: Security Awareness and Training

Security awareness is a crucial element of any organization's cybersecurity strategy, as it empowers individuals within the organization to play an active role in safeguarding sensitive information and digital assets.

In today's interconnected and digitally driven world, where cyber threats continually evolve and adapt, security awareness serves as a vital defense against cyberattacks.

While technology and security measures are essential components of cybersecurity, human factors play a significant role in determining an organization's overall security posture.

Cybersecurity incidents often occur due to human errors, such as falling victim to phishing emails, using weak passwords, or inadvertently disclosing sensitive information.

By raising awareness and educating employees, contractors, and other stakeholders about cybersecurity risks and best practices, organizations can reduce the likelihood of these errors.

One of the key aspects of security awareness is educating individuals about the various forms of cyber threats they may encounter.

This includes phishing attacks, malware infections, social engineering tactics, ransomware, and more.

When individuals understand the types of threats they may face, they are better equipped to recognize and respond to them effectively.

Security awareness programs also emphasize the importance of strong password practices.

Passwords serve as the first line of defense against unauthorized access to accounts and systems.

Educating individuals about the significance of creating complex, unique passwords and regularly changing them helps protect against password-related security incidents.

Another critical area of focus in security awareness is email security.

Phishing attacks, which involve deceptive emails that trick recipients into revealing sensitive information or clicking on malicious links, remain a prevalent threat.

Training individuals to recognize phishing attempts and follow best practices when handling email can significantly reduce the risk of falling victim to such attacks.

Beyond email security, security awareness programs cover safe web browsing practices and the importance of keeping software and systems up to date.

Outdated software often contains vulnerabilities that attackers can exploit, so timely updates and patches are essential.

Furthermore, security awareness emphasizes the need for individuals to exercise caution when sharing information online and on social media.

Cybercriminals often gather information from public sources to craft convincing social engineering attacks.

By understanding the risks of oversharing and practicing discretion, individuals can protect their personal and professional information.

In addition to educating individuals about cybersecurity risks, security awareness programs promote a culture of cybersecurity within organizations.

This culture encourages individuals to take responsibility for their own cybersecurity and the security of the organization as a whole.

It emphasizes the shared goal of protecting sensitive data and assets, fostering a sense of collective responsibility.

Security awareness is not limited to employees; it extends to all individuals who interact with an organization's systems and data.

This includes contractors, vendors, and partners who may have access to sensitive information.

By including these external stakeholders in security awareness initiatives, organizations ensure a more comprehensive approach to cybersecurity.

Moreover, security awareness is an ongoing process.

Cyber threats evolve continuously, and new tactics and vulnerabilities emerge regularly.

Therefore, security awareness programs should be dynamic and adaptable, reflecting the current threat landscape.

Regular training, updates, and reminders are essential to keep individuals informed and engaged in cybersecurity efforts.

Effective security awareness programs leverage various training methods, including e-learning modules, workshops, simulations, and quizzes.

These methods engage individuals in interactive learning experiences that reinforce key cybersecurity principles and practices.

Moreover, security awareness programs often include reporting mechanisms that allow individuals to report suspicious activities or incidents promptly.

Timely reporting enables incident response teams to take action swiftly, preventing or mitigating potential security incidents.

To gauge the effectiveness of security awareness efforts, organizations may conduct simulated phishing campaigns and assess how individuals respond to mock phishing emails.

This provides valuable insights into the organization's overall readiness and highlights areas that require further attention and training.

In summary, security awareness is a fundamental pillar of modern cybersecurity strategies.

It empowers individuals within organizations to recognize, prevent, and respond to cyber threats effectively.

By educating and engaging employees, contractors, and stakeholders in a culture of cybersecurity, organizations can significantly enhance their overall security posture and reduce the risk of cybersecurity incidents.

Designing effective security training programs is essential for organizations to build a workforce that is well-prepared to mitigate cyber risks and protect sensitive information.

These training programs are crucial in an era where cyber threats are ever-evolving, and human errors continue to be a significant factor in security incidents.

To create effective security training, it's essential to start by understanding the specific needs and risks of your organization.

This requires a thorough assessment of your organization's current security posture, the types of data you handle, and the regulatory requirements you must meet.

By identifying your unique security challenges, you can tailor your training programs to address the most critical areas.

Security training should cover a broad range of topics, from basic cybersecurity concepts to specific threats and incident response procedures.

It should be designed to cater to different roles within the organization, as employees in various positions have distinct security responsibilities.

A crucial aspect of effective security training is making it engaging and relevant to the audience.

Monotonous, one-size-fits-all training modules can be ineffective and lead to disengagement.

To overcome this challenge, consider using interactive, scenario-based training modules that simulate real-world situations.

This allows participants to apply their knowledge and practice making the right decisions in a safe environment.

Moreover, it's essential to keep the content up to date to reflect the latest cyber threats and security best practices.

Cybersecurity is a constantly evolving field, and training materials that were relevant a year ago may no longer be applicable.

Regularly review and refresh the training content to ensure that it remains accurate and aligns with current threat landscapes.

Another key consideration is the delivery method of your training programs.

Traditional classroom-style training may not be suitable for all employees, especially in today's remote and diverse work environments.

Consider using a blended approach, incorporating e-learning modules, webinars, and in-person workshops to accommodate different learning preferences and schedules.

Additionally, consider providing training in small, digestible segments rather than overwhelming participants with long, information-heavy sessions.

Effective security training programs also emphasize the importance of hands-on learning and practical exercises.

This allows participants to apply what they've learned in a controlled setting, helping them build confidence and competence in their security skills.

Simulated phishing exercises, for example, can help employees recognize and respond to phishing attempts effectively.

Furthermore, training programs should promote a culture of cybersecurity within the organization.

This includes encouraging employees to take ownership of their security responsibilities and fostering a sense of shared accountability.

Incorporate scenarios and examples that are relevant to the organization's specific industry and environment.

This makes the training more relatable to participants, as they can see how security principles apply to their daily work.

Security training programs should also provide clear guidance on reporting security incidents.

Participants should know how to report suspicious activities, breaches, or policy violations promptly.

Encourage a culture of transparency and emphasize that reporting incidents is a crucial part of the organization's security efforts.

Metrics and assessments play a significant role in gauging the effectiveness of security training programs.

Regularly evaluate the impact of your training efforts by measuring key performance indicators (KPIs), such as incident response times, incident detection rates, and employee awareness.

Conduct assessments or quizzes to ensure that participants have grasped the essential security concepts and practices.

Feedback from participants is valuable for improving training programs.

Gather their input and suggestions to identify areas that may need further refinement or clarification.

Effective security training programs should also incorporate elements of gamification to make learning enjoyable.

Consider using leaderboards, badges, or rewards for achieving specific training milestones or demonstrating exceptional security practices.

This can motivate participants to actively engage in the training and compete with their peers in a positive way.

Furthermore, consider providing ongoing training and awareness initiatives.

Cybersecurity is not a one-time effort but an ongoing commitment.

Regularly reinforce security concepts and remind employees of the importance of staying vigilant.

Create a culture where security is embedded in the organization's DNA, and employees understand that their actions directly impact the organization's overall security.

In summary, designing effective security training programs is a critical aspect of a robust cybersecurity strategy.

These programs should be tailored to the organization's specific needs and risks, engaging, relevant, and up-to-date.

By promoting a culture of cybersecurity, encouraging hands-on learning, and regularly assessing the impact of training efforts, organizations can build a resilient workforce capable of defending against cyber threats effectively.

Chapter 9: Security Policies and Compliance

Developing security policies and procedures is a critical step in establishing a strong cybersecurity framework for any organization.

These policies and procedures provide the foundation for implementing security measures, managing risks, and ensuring compliance with regulatory requirements.

A well-defined set of security policies communicates an organization's commitment to protecting its data and assets, and it serves as a guide for employees, contractors, and partners to follow.

One of the fundamental aspects of developing security policies is defining the scope and objectives of the policies.

This involves identifying the assets and data that need protection, the potential threats and vulnerabilities, and the specific goals the policies aim to achieve.

Clear objectives help ensure that the policies are aligned with the organization's security strategy and business goals.

It's important to involve key stakeholders from various departments when developing security policies and procedures.

This collaboration ensures that the policies are comprehensive, relevant to different parts of the organization, and well-understood by those who will be responsible for implementing them.

When crafting security policies, consider the regulatory environment in which your organization operates.

Different industries and regions have specific legal and compliance requirements that must be addressed in the policies.

By staying informed about relevant regulations, you can develop policies that help your organization maintain compliance.

Security policies should be written in a clear and concise manner, avoiding technical jargon and ambiguity.

The goal is to make the policies accessible and understandable to all employees, regardless of their technical expertise.

Using plain language ensures that employees can easily comprehend their responsibilities and the expected security practices.

To enhance the effectiveness of security policies, consider categorizing them into different levels or tiers.

For example, you might have high-level policies that provide a broad overview of security principles and objectives, followed by more detailed operational procedures and guidelines.

This tiered approach allows employees to access information relevant to their roles and responsibilities.

Security policies should address a wide range of topics, including data protection, access control, incident response, encryption, and acceptable use of technology resources.

Each policy should outline specific rules and guidelines related to the topic and provide information on how to report violations or security incidents.

It's essential to keep security policies up to date to reflect the evolving threat landscape and changes within the organization.

Regularly review and revise policies as needed, and ensure that employees are made aware of any updates.

Training and awareness programs play a crucial role in ensuring that employees understand and adhere to security policies.

Effective training programs educate employees on the policies, explain their significance, and provide practical guidance on how to implement them in their daily tasks.

Furthermore, employees should receive regular reminders and updates on security policies to reinforce their importance.

Security policies should define roles and responsibilities within the organization regarding security.

For example, they should specify who is responsible for access control, who should handle incident response, and who should oversee compliance with the policies.

Clear delineation of responsibilities helps ensure that everyone understands their role in maintaining security.

To encourage compliance with security policies, organizations should establish a framework for monitoring and enforcing them.

This may include regular audits, access reviews, and automated security controls that help detect and prevent policy violations.

Enforcement mechanisms should be clearly outlined in the policies, including potential consequences for non-compliance.

Moreover, organizations should establish a process for employees to report security concerns or incidents confidentially.

This encourages open communication and allows for the timely resolution of security issues.

As technology evolves, organizations must adapt their security policies and procedures to address new threats and emerging technologies.

For example, policies related to remote work and bring-your-own-device (BYOD) should be regularly updated to reflect the changing landscape of remote work and mobile technologies.

Additionally, organizations should have an incident response plan in place to address security incidents when they occur.

This plan should be closely aligned with the organization's security policies and procedures, outlining the steps to take when a security incident is detected.

Developing security policies and procedures is an ongoing process that requires continuous improvement and adaptation.

Regularly assess the effectiveness of your policies, gather feedback from employees, and adjust them accordingly.

Consider conducting security awareness campaigns to reinforce the importance of security practices outlined in the policies.

In summary, developing security policies and procedures is a critical element of a robust cybersecurity strategy.

Well-defined policies help guide employees in maintaining a secure environment, protect sensitive data, and ensure compliance with regulations.

By involving stakeholders, regularly reviewing and updating policies, and fostering a culture of security, organizations can strengthen their overall security posture and reduce the risk of security incidents.

Compliance frameworks and regulations are essential components of the cybersecurity landscape, providing organizations with guidance and requirements to ensure the protection of sensitive data and the mitigation of cybersecurity risks.

In today's interconnected world, where data breaches and cyber threats are on the rise, compliance frameworks and regulations play a vital role in helping organizations establish and maintain effective cybersecurity practices.

These frameworks are designed to serve as blueprints for organizations to build their cybersecurity programs, addressing various aspects of information security, data privacy, and risk management.

One of the most well-known compliance frameworks is the Payment Card Industry Data Security Standard (PCI DSS).

PCI DSS outlines security requirements for organizations that handle credit card transactions, aiming to protect cardholder data and prevent data breaches.

Organizations that accept credit card payments must adhere to PCI DSS to ensure the security of payment card information.

Another widely recognized compliance framework is the Health Insurance Portability and Accountability Act (HIPAA) in the United States.

HIPAA sets standards for the protection of electronic protected health information (ePHI) and mandates the implementation of security controls to safeguard patients' sensitive medical records.

Organizations in the healthcare industry must comply with HIPAA to ensure the privacy and security of patient data.

The General Data Protection Regulation (GDPR), established in the European Union, is a comprehensive data protection regulation that governs the processing of personal data.

GDPR imposes strict requirements on organizations regarding data collection, storage, and handling, as well as notification and consent procedures.

Companies that process personal data of EU citizens must adhere to GDPR's stringent data protection rules.

The National Institute of Standards and Technology (NIST) Cybersecurity Framework is a widely adopted framework in the United States that provides guidelines and best practices for managing and reducing cybersecurity risk.

NIST's framework focuses on five core functions: identify, protect, detect, respond, and recover, providing a structured approach to enhancing cybersecurity posture.

The International Organization for Standardization (ISO) 27001 is a globally recognized standard for information security management systems (ISMS).

ISO 27001 outlines a systematic approach to managing information security risks and requires organizations to establish a framework to protect their data assets effectively.

These compliance frameworks and regulations serve as valuable resources for organizations, helping them establish a strong foundation for cybersecurity and data protection.

In addition to industry-specific regulations and standards, organizations may also be subject to regional or country-specific laws governing data privacy and security.

For example, the California Consumer Privacy Act (CCPA) in the United States imposes strict requirements on organizations that handle the personal information of California residents.

Similarly, the Personal Data Protection Act (PDPA) in Singapore mandates the responsible and transparent handling of personal data.

To navigate this complex landscape of compliance requirements, organizations often engage in a process of assessing their current cybersecurity practices and aligning them with the relevant frameworks and regulations.

This involves identifying areas where the organization may fall short of compliance requirements and taking steps to address any gaps.

Organizations may need to implement additional security controls, enhance data protection measures, and establish robust incident response procedures to meet compliance standards.

Regular audits and assessments are essential to ensure ongoing compliance with the chosen frameworks and regulations.

External auditors or internal compliance teams may conduct assessments to evaluate the organization's adherence to security controls and practices.

These assessments help organizations identify areas for improvement and demonstrate their commitment to cybersecurity to regulators, customers, and partners.

Maintaining compliance is an ongoing effort, as cybersecurity threats and regulatory landscapes evolve.

Organizations must stay vigilant, continuously monitor their security posture, and adapt their cybersecurity programs to address emerging risks.

Additionally, organizations should foster a culture of compliance awareness among employees, ensuring that everyone understands their role in maintaining data security and adhering to relevant regulations.

Training and awareness programs can help employees recognize the importance of compliance and their responsibility in protecting sensitive data.

In summary, compliance frameworks and regulations play a crucial role in shaping the cybersecurity landscape.

These frameworks provide organizations with guidance and requirements to establish robust cybersecurity practices and protect sensitive data.

By aligning with the relevant frameworks and regulations, organizations can enhance their cybersecurity posture, build trust with customers, and demonstrate their commitment to data security and privacy.

Chapter 10: Emerging Trends in Operational Security

The current threat landscape in the world of cybersecurity is characterized by a constantly evolving and highly dynamic environment where cyber threats and attacks continue to proliferate at an alarming rate.

Organizations and individuals alike face an ever-increasing array of threats that target their digital assets, sensitive data, and online presence.

One of the prominent threats in the current landscape is the prevalence of phishing attacks, where cybercriminals craft deceptive emails, websites, or messages to trick users into revealing personal information, credentials, or financial details.

Phishing attacks have become more sophisticated, often using social engineering techniques and highly convincing disguises to lure victims.

Ransomware attacks have also surged in recent years, with cybercriminals encrypting an organization's data and demanding a ransom for its release.

These attacks not only disrupt operations but also pose significant financial and reputational risks to victims.

Furthermore, supply chain attacks have gained prominence, with attackers infiltrating an organization through vulnerabilities in their supply chain partners.

By compromising a trusted partner, attackers can gain access to an organization's networks and systems, making these attacks challenging to detect and mitigate.

State-sponsored cyberattacks have continued to be a major concern in the current threat landscape.

Nation-states and state-sponsored threat actors engage in cyber espionage, intellectual property theft, and disruptive attacks, targeting both government entities and private sector organizations.

Advanced persistent threats (APTs) are often associated with state-sponsored actors who conduct long-term, stealthy campaigns to infiltrate and maintain access to their targets.

Moreover, the rise of the Internet of Things (IoT) has introduced new security challenges, as poorly secured IoT devices provide entry points for cyber attackers.

These devices, ranging from smart thermostats to industrial control systems, are susceptible to exploitation, potentially leading to critical infrastructure vulnerabilities.

The proliferation of remote work and the adoption of cloud services have expanded the attack surface, as organizations rely on remote access solutions and cloud infrastructure.

This has led to an increase in attacks targeting remote workers, cloud-based assets, and misconfigured cloud environments.

Additionally, cryptojacking attacks have become more prevalent, where attackers use a victim's computing resources to mine cryptocurrencies without their knowledge or consent.

These attacks can slow down systems, consume energy, and lead to financial losses for victims.

Social engineering attacks, such as pretexting, baiting, and tailgating, remain a significant threat in the current landscape, relying on manipulating human psychology to deceive individuals into divulging sensitive information or granting unauthorized access.

Business email compromise (BEC) attacks, a type of social engineering, involve compromising email accounts to impersonate trusted contacts and initiate fraudulent transactions or data theft.

In response to the evolving threat landscape, organizations must adopt a proactive and multi-layered approach to cybersecurity.

This includes implementing robust security measures such as firewalls, intrusion detection systems, and advanced threat detection solutions to monitor network traffic for suspicious activities.

Regular patch management and system updates are essential to address vulnerabilities that attackers exploit.

Moreover, organizations must invest in employee training and awareness programs to educate staff about the latest threats and how to recognize and respond to them.

Implementing strong access controls, multi-factor authentication, and encryption helps protect sensitive data and prevent unauthorized access.

Cybersecurity incident response plans should be in place, enabling organizations to react swiftly and effectively when a security incident occurs.

Collaboration with cybersecurity information-sharing communities and the use of threat intelligence feeds can provide valuable insights into emerging threats and attack patterns.

Moreover, organizations should conduct regular security assessments and penetration testing to identify and remediate vulnerabilities proactively.

Third-party risk assessments are crucial to evaluate the security posture of supply chain partners and vendors.

In summary, the current threat landscape presents a multitude of cybersecurity challenges, with attackers becoming more sophisticated and organizations facing a wider attack surface.

To navigate this landscape successfully, organizations must prioritize cybersecurity, stay informed about emerging threats, and implement a comprehensive security strategy that encompasses people, processes, and technology.

By adopting a proactive and adaptive approach to cybersecurity, organizations can enhance their resilience and protect their digital assets in an increasingly perilous digital world.

The landscape of cybersecurity is continually evolving, and as we look to the future, we can anticipate a range of challenges and innovations that will shape the field.

One of the foremost challenges on the horizon is the increasing sophistication of cyber threats, with attackers employing advanced tactics, techniques, and procedures to evade detection and compromise systems.

These sophisticated threats are often nation-state-sponsored, organized crime-driven, or conducted by highly skilled hacking groups, posing significant risks to organizations and individuals alike.

Additionally, the expanding attack surface brought about by the proliferation of Internet of Things (IoT) devices, cloud technologies, and remote work will continue to challenge security professionals.

As more devices become interconnected, the potential vulnerabilities and entry points for cyber attackers grow, demanding robust security measures and strategies.

Furthermore, privacy concerns are likely to intensify, as individuals become increasingly aware of the importance of protecting their personal data in an era of rampant data breaches and cyber threats.

Regulatory frameworks and consumer expectations are pushing organizations to prioritize data privacy and implement stringent data protection measures.

In response to these challenges, the cybersecurity community is poised for numerous innovations and advancements.

Artificial Intelligence (AI) and machine learning will play a pivotal role in improving threat detection and response capabilities.

These technologies can analyze vast amounts of data in real-time, identifying anomalies and patterns that may indicate cyberattacks or security breaches.

Automation will also become more prevalent, allowing for rapid incident response and threat mitigation.

The integration of AI-driven security solutions into organizations' cybersecurity strategies will become increasingly important in the years ahead.

Moreover, the development of quantum computing presents both opportunities and challenges in the realm of cybersecurity.

Quantum computers have the potential to break current encryption algorithms, rendering traditional cryptographic methods obsolete.

As a result, the cybersecurity community is working on quantum-resistant encryption techniques to ensure data security in a post-quantum world.

Cloud-native security solutions will continue to evolve, as organizations rely more on cloud services and platforms for their operations.

Cloud security innovations will focus on protecting data in transit and at rest, ensuring the integrity and availability of cloud-hosted resources.

In addition to technological advancements, a crucial aspect of future cybersecurity is the human element.

Social engineering attacks, such as phishing and pretexting, will remain prevalent, requiring ongoing education and awareness programs to empower individuals to recognize and resist these manipulative tactics.

The development of a cybersecurity workforce with diverse skills and expertise will be essential in addressing the evolving threat landscape.

This includes not only technical experts but also professionals skilled in risk management, compliance, and legal aspects of cybersecurity.

Collaboration and information sharing among organizations, government agencies, and international cybersecurity communities will be vital in countering global cyber threats.

Threat intelligence sharing platforms and coordinated response efforts will help identify and respond to cyberattacks more effectively.

Furthermore, organizations will increasingly adopt a zero-trust security model, which assumes that threats may exist both outside and inside the network perimeter.

This approach requires continuous verification of users and devices, regardless of their location, to minimize the risk of unauthorized access.

Blockchain technology may also find applications in cybersecurity, offering enhanced transparency and trust in data transactions and identity verification.

Decentralized identity systems and secure data storage on the blockchain could provide new ways to protect sensitive information.

Simultaneously, the security industry will continue to face challenges related to the rapid pace of technological innovation.

Emerging technologies, such as 5G networks, edge computing, and artificial intelligence, bring new cybersecurity considerations that demand adaptation and preparedness.

Furthermore, the growing interconnectivity of critical infrastructure systems, including power grids and transportation networks, raises concerns about their vulnerability to cyberattacks.

Securing these critical systems will require a concerted effort from governments and organizations to develop robust defenses against potential threats.

In summary, the future of cybersecurity promises a mix of challenges and innovations.

Sophisticated cyber threats, an expanding attack surface, and heightened privacy concerns will test the resilience of organizations and individuals.

However, advancements in AI, quantum-resistant encryption, cloud-native security, and a strong cybersecurity workforce offer opportunities to strengthen cybersecurity defenses.

Collaboration, information sharing, and a proactive, adaptive approach will be essential in addressing the evolving threat landscape and ensuring a secure digital future.

BOOK 2
MASTERING INCIDENT RESPONSE
STRATEGIES FOR BLUE TEAMS

ROB BOTWRIGHT

Chapter 1: Introduction to Incident Response

Incident response is a fundamental aspect of cybersecurity, essential for effectively mitigating the impact of security incidents when they occur.

An incident response plan outlines the procedures and processes an organization follows when a security incident is detected.

These incidents can range from data breaches and malware infections to unauthorized access and denial-of-service attacks.

The primary goals of incident response are to minimize damage, reduce recovery time and costs, and ensure the organization can return to normal operations as quickly as possible.

A well-prepared incident response plan is a crucial component of an organization's overall cybersecurity strategy.

The first step in incident response is preparation, which involves creating an incident response team, defining roles and responsibilities, and developing an incident response plan.

The incident response team typically includes individuals from various departments, such as IT, legal, public relations, and management, to ensure a coordinated and effective response.

Roles within the team may include an incident commander, technical analysts, legal counsel, and communication coordinators.

The incident response plan should be tailored to the organization's specific needs and risks, taking into account the types of threats it may face and the criticality of its systems and data.

Once the incident response plan is in place, the next phase is detection and identification.

This involves monitoring systems and networks for signs of suspicious or unauthorized activity and quickly identifying potential security incidents.

Organizations may use security information and event management (SIEM) systems, intrusion detection systems (IDS), and other monitoring tools to aid in this process.

The goal is to detect incidents as early as possible to initiate a rapid response.

When a security incident is detected, the incident response team must assess the situation to determine the nature and scope of the incident.

This assessment includes identifying the affected systems and data, understanding the attacker's tactics and objectives, and evaluating the potential impact on the organization.

Timely and accurate assessment is critical in determining the appropriate response actions.

Once the incident has been assessed, containment and eradication are the next steps in the incident response process.

Containment involves isolating the affected systems to prevent further damage and spreading of the incident.

Eradication focuses on identifying and removing the root cause of the incident, such as malware, unauthorized access points, or vulnerabilities.

The goal is to eliminate the threat and prevent it from recurring.

After containment and eradication, organizations must focus on recovery.

Recovery involves restoring affected systems and data to normal operations.

This may include restoring data from backups, patching vulnerabilities, and ensuring that systems are secure before bringing them back online.

The incident response team should work closely with IT and system administrators during this phase to minimize downtime and disruption.

Communication is a critical aspect of incident response.

Organizations must have clear communication plans in place to inform stakeholders about the incident, its impact, and the steps being taken to address it.

Communication may include notifying customers, partners, regulators, and law enforcement if necessary.

Transparency and timely updates are essential to maintain trust and credibility.

In parallel with containment, eradication, and recovery efforts, organizations should conduct a thorough post-incident analysis or debriefing.

This analysis helps identify the lessons learned from the incident, assess the effectiveness of the incident response plan, and make improvements for future incidents.

The incident response team should document the incident, including the actions taken, communication logs, and any forensic evidence collected.

This documentation is crucial for legal and regulatory purposes and for continuous improvement of the incident response process.

In addition to post-incident analysis, organizations should conduct regular incident response drills and exercises.

These exercises help the incident response team practice their roles and responsibilities, test the effectiveness of the incident response plan, and identify areas for improvement.

Simulating different types of incidents, such as data breaches, malware infections, or insider threats, provides valuable experience and prepares the team for real-world scenarios.

It's important to note that incident response is not a one-time activity but an ongoing process.

Organizations must continuously monitor for threats, update their incident response plans, and adapt to new attack tactics and technologies.

The incident response team should stay current with the latest cybersecurity trends and participate in training and certification programs to enhance their skills.

In summary, incident response is a critical component of cybersecurity, designed to minimize the impact of security incidents and ensure a rapid return to normal operations.

A well-prepared incident response plan, a trained incident response team, and effective communication are essential for managing security incidents effectively.

In the complex and ever-evolving landscape of cybersecurity, incident response plays a pivotal role in safeguarding organizations against cyber threats.

Incident response is not merely a reactive process; it is a well-defined and proactive strategy that aims to mitigate the impact of security incidents when they inevitably occur.

Security incidents encompass a wide range of events, from data breaches and malware infections to unauthorized access attempts and denial-of-service attacks.

The primary objective of incident response is to minimize damage, reduce recovery time, and facilitate the organization's return to normal operations.

An incident response plan is a fundamental component of any organization's cybersecurity strategy.

This plan serves as a roadmap, outlining the procedures and processes to follow when a security incident is detected.

Creating an effective incident response plan begins with assembling a dedicated incident response team.

This team should comprise individuals from various departments, including IT, legal, public relations, and management, to ensure a holistic and coordinated response.

Within the incident response team, specific roles and responsibilities are defined to ensure that each member knows their tasks and functions during an incident.

These roles may include an incident commander, technical analysts, legal counsel, and communication coordinators.

A crucial aspect of incident response planning is customization to meet the organization's unique needs and risks.

Consideration should be given to the types of threats the organization may face and the criticality of its systems and data.

Tailoring the plan to address these specific concerns is essential for an effective response.

The incident response process typically consists of several phases, beginning with preparation.

Preparation involves the creation of the incident response plan, the formation of the response team, and the development of strategies for managing incidents effectively.

Having a plan in place and a team ready to act can significantly reduce the impact of a security incident.

The next phase is detection and identification.

Organizations must monitor their systems and networks diligently to detect signs of suspicious or unauthorized activity.

This phase requires the use of security information and event management (SIEM) systems, intrusion detection systems (IDS), and other monitoring tools.

The goal is to identify security incidents as early as possible to initiate a swift response.

Once a security incident is detected, the incident response team proceeds to assess the situation.

This assessment involves determining the nature and scope of the incident, identifying affected systems and data, and evaluating the potential impact on the organization.

A timely and accurate assessment is crucial for determining the appropriate response actions.

Containment and eradication are the subsequent phases of incident response.

Containment entails isolating the affected systems to prevent further damage and the spread of the incident.

Eradication focuses on identifying and removing the root cause of the incident, such as malware, unauthorized access points, or vulnerabilities.

The goal is to eliminate the threat and prevent it from recurring.

Following containment and eradication, the organization moves on to the recovery phase.

Recovery involves restoring affected systems and data to normal operations.

This may include restoring data from backups, patching vulnerabilities, and ensuring that systems are secure before bringing them back online.

Effective communication is a critical aspect of incident response.

Organizations must have clear communication plans in place to inform stakeholders about the incident, its impact, and the steps being taken to address it.

Transparency and timely updates are essential to maintain trust and credibility.

While these phases of incident response address the technical aspects, a thorough post-incident analysis is equally important.

This analysis helps organizations identify lessons learned from the incident, assess the effectiveness of the incident response plan, and make improvements for future incidents.

Documentation of the incident, including actions taken, communication logs, and forensic evidence, is crucial for legal and regulatory purposes and for continuous improvement. In parallel with post-incident analysis, organizations should conduct regular incident response drills and exercises. These exercises allow the incident response team to practice their roles, test the effectiveness of the plan, and identify areas for improvement.

Simulating different types of incidents, such as data breaches or malware infections, provides valuable experience and prepares the team for real-world scenarios.

It's important to note that incident response is not a one-time activity but an ongoing process.

Organizations must continuously monitor for threats, update their incident response plans, and adapt to new attack tactics and technologies.

The incident response team should stay current with the latest cybersecurity trends and participate in training and certification programs to enhance their skills.

In summary, incident response is a vital component of cybersecurity, designed to minimize the impact of security incidents and ensure a rapid return to normal operations.

A well-prepared incident response plan, a trained incident response team, and effective communication are essential for managing security incidents effectively.

Chapter 2: The Incident Response Framework

To effectively grasp the concept of an incident response framework, it's essential to recognize that cybersecurity incidents are inevitable in today's digital landscape.

These incidents can vary in severity and impact, ranging from minor security breaches to major data breaches with far-reaching consequences.

An incident response framework provides a structured and systematic approach to dealing with these incidents.

At its core, an incident response framework serves as a blueprint, guiding organizations through the steps necessary to identify, manage, and mitigate the effects of a security incident.

The framework's primary goal is to minimize damage, reduce recovery time, and restore normal operations as swiftly as possible.

One widely adopted incident response framework is based on four key phases: preparation, detection and analysis, containment, and recovery.

The first phase, preparation, is the foundation of an effective incident response framework.

During this phase, organizations lay the groundwork for incident management by establishing the incident response team, defining their roles and responsibilities, and creating an incident response plan.

The incident response team typically consists of individuals from various departments, such as IT, legal, public relations, and management, to ensure a comprehensive response.

Roles within the team may include an incident commander, technical analysts, legal counsel, and communication coordinators.

The incident response plan outlines how the organization will respond to different types of incidents and should be customized to address specific risks and needs.

Once the preparation phase is complete, the organization moves on to the detection and analysis phase.

In this phase, the focus is on identifying security incidents as early as possible.

Continuous monitoring of systems and networks for signs of suspicious or unauthorized activity is a crucial part of this phase.

Security information and event management (SIEM) systems, intrusion detection systems (IDS), and other monitoring tools play a vital role in detecting incidents.

When a potential security incident is identified, the incident response team conducts a thorough analysis.

This analysis aims to determine the nature and scope of the incident, identify affected systems and data, and assess the potential impact on the organization.

A swift and accurate assessment is essential for determining the appropriate response actions.

Once the incident has been analyzed, the containment phase begins.

Containment involves taking immediate actions to stop the incident from spreading further and causing additional damage.

This may include isolating affected systems from the network, blocking malicious network traffic, or disabling compromised accounts.

The goal is to prevent the incident from escalating while the organization investigates and eradicates the root cause.

After containment, the organization moves on to the eradication phase.

Eradication focuses on identifying and eliminating the source of the incident, such as malware, vulnerabilities, or unauthorized access points.

This phase often involves deep forensic analysis to understand how the incident occurred and to ensure that all traces of the threat are removed.

It's crucial to eradicate the threat completely to prevent it from recurring.

With the threat eradicated, the organization enters the recovery phase.

Recovery involves restoring affected systems and data to normal operations.

This may include restoring data from backups, applying patches to vulnerabilities, and verifying the security of systems before bringing them back online.

Effective recovery efforts are essential to minimize downtime and disruptions.

Throughout these phases, communication is a critical element of the incident response framework.

Organizations must have clear communication plans in place to inform stakeholders about the incident, its impact, and the steps being taken to address it.

Transparency and timely updates are vital to maintain trust and credibility.

In parallel with the incident response phases, organizations should conduct a comprehensive post-incident analysis.

This analysis helps organizations identify lessons learned from the incident, evaluate the effectiveness of their incident response plan, and make improvements for future incidents.

Documentation of the incident, including actions taken, communication logs, and forensic evidence, is essential for legal and regulatory purposes and for continuous improvement.

Regular incident response drills and exercises are another critical component of an effective incident response framework.

These exercises allow the incident response team to practice their roles, test the effectiveness of the plan, and identify areas for improvement.

Simulating various types of incidents, such as data breaches or malware infections, provides valuable experience and prepares the team for real-world scenarios.

In summary, understanding the incident response framework is crucial for organizations aiming to effectively manage cybersecurity incidents.

It provides a structured and systematic approach to dealing with incidents, helping organizations minimize damage, reduce recovery time, and restore normal operations swiftly.

A well-prepared incident response framework, a trained incident response team, and effective communication are essential for managing security incidents effectively.

In delving into the key components of the incident response framework, it becomes evident that each element plays a crucial role in orchestrating an effective response to security incidents.

First and foremost, the incident response team stands at the core of this framework, as it's composed of individuals who bring diverse expertise and skills to the table.

This team is responsible for implementing the incident response plan, and their roles and responsibilities are well-defined to ensure a coordinated effort.

Among the roles within the incident response team, the incident commander assumes a pivotal role in overseeing the response efforts, making critical decisions, and ensuring that the plan is executed efficiently.

Technical analysts, on the other hand, are tasked with investigating and analyzing the incident, seeking to understand its scope and nature.

Legal counsel within the team provides crucial guidance on legal matters, ensuring that the organization complies with relevant laws and regulations during the response process.

Communication coordinators play an essential role in keeping stakeholders informed, maintaining transparency, and managing the organization's reputation.

The incident response plan itself is a fundamental component of the framework, serving as the roadmap that guides the organization's response efforts.

This plan should be meticulously developed, taking into account the organization's specific needs, risks, and objectives.

It outlines the procedures and processes for responding to various types of incidents, providing a structured approach that minimizes confusion and ensures that critical steps are not overlooked.

Customization of the plan is key, as it allows organizations to tailor their response strategies to address the unique threats they may face.

The plan encompasses a wide range of response procedures, including incident identification, assessment, containment, eradication, recovery, and communication.

Additionally, it often incorporates decision-making criteria, escalation procedures, and incident categorization guidelines to streamline the response process.

Monitoring and detection mechanisms represent another critical component of the incident response framework.

Organizations must employ continuous monitoring of their systems and networks to detect any signs of suspicious or unauthorized activity.

This proactive approach to detection enables organizations to identify security incidents as early as possible, facilitating a rapid response.

Various tools and technologies are employed for this purpose, including security information and event management (SIEM) systems, intrusion detection systems (IDS), and anomaly detection solutions.

These tools help organizations monitor network traffic, system logs, and other data sources for indicators of compromise or potential threats.

When a potential incident is detected, the incident response team springs into action to assess the situation.

This assessment phase is essential for understanding the incident's nature and scope, evaluating its potential impact, and determining the appropriate response actions.

The goal is to gather as much information as possible to make informed decisions and develop an effective response strategy.

Accurate assessment is critical in ensuring that resources are allocated efficiently and that the incident is handled appropriately.

Containment and eradication procedures are key components of the incident response framework, as they are aimed at stopping the incident from spreading further and eliminating its root cause.

Containment measures may involve isolating affected systems, blocking malicious network traffic, or disabling compromised accounts to prevent the incident's escalation.

Eradication efforts focus on identifying and removing the source of the incident, such as malware, unauthorized access points, or vulnerabilities.

In some cases, deep forensic analysis may be necessary to fully understand the incident and ensure that all traces of the threat are eradicated.

Once containment and eradication are complete, the organization proceeds to the recovery phase.

Recovery efforts are aimed at restoring affected systems and data to normal operations, minimizing downtime and disruptions.

This phase may involve data restoration from backups, patching vulnerabilities, and thorough testing to ensure that systems are secure before they are brought back online.

Effective recovery is essential for an organization to return to business as usual swiftly.

Effective communication is a cornerstone of the incident response framework, as it ensures that stakeholders are kept informed and that the organization's reputation is managed effectively.

Organizations must have clear communication plans in place to address various aspects of the incident, including notifying affected parties, providing updates on the incident's progress, and coordinating with law enforcement and regulatory authorities if necessary.

Transparency and timely communication are vital in maintaining trust and credibility during a security incident.

Post-incident analysis and documentation represent a critical aspect of the incident response framework.

After an incident is resolved, organizations should conduct a thorough analysis to identify lessons learned, assess the effectiveness of the incident response plan, and make improvements for future incidents.

Documentation of the incident, including actions taken, communication logs, and forensic evidence collected, is crucial for legal and regulatory purposes and for continuous improvement.

Regular incident response drills and exercises are instrumental in ensuring that the incident response team is well-prepared to handle real-world incidents.

These exercises allow the team to practice their roles, test the effectiveness of the plan, and identify areas for improvement.

Simulating different types of incidents, such as data breaches or malware infections, provides valuable experience and ensures that the team can respond effectively in challenging situations.

In summary, the key components of the incident response framework form a comprehensive and structured approach to addressing security incidents.

The incident response team, incident response plan, monitoring and detection mechanisms, assessment, containment and eradication procedures, recovery efforts, communication plans, post-incident analysis, and regular drills all contribute to a robust framework that enables organizations to effectively manage and mitigate the impact of security incidents.

Chapter 3: Identifying and Classifying Incidents

When it comes to identifying security incidents, organizations employ a variety of methods and techniques to detect potential threats and unauthorized activities within their networks and systems.

One of the primary methods for identifying security incidents is through continuous monitoring of network traffic and system logs.

By analyzing network traffic patterns and monitoring system logs for unusual or suspicious activities, organizations can quickly spot anomalies that may indicate a security incident.

This includes looking for patterns such as repeated login failures, unexpected data transfers, or unusual system access.

Security Information and Event Management (SIEM) systems are commonly used for this purpose, as they centralize log data and provide real-time analysis.

Intrusion Detection Systems (IDS) and Intrusion Prevention Systems (IPS) are also employed to identify and alert organizations to potentially malicious activities.

These systems analyze network traffic for known attack signatures and patterns, raising alerts when they detect suspicious behavior.

Additionally, anomaly detection systems can help identify security incidents by comparing current network behavior to historical data and flagging deviations.

Another method for identifying security incidents involves the use of endpoint detection and response (EDR) solutions.

These solutions are installed on individual endpoints, such as laptops and servers, and continuously monitor the behavior of these devices.

They can identify unusual or malicious activities on the endpoints, such as the execution of suspicious processes, changes to system files, or attempts to exploit vulnerabilities.

Furthermore, organizations often employ security event correlation, which involves aggregating and correlating data from various sources to identify potential security incidents.

By combining information from multiple systems and logs, security teams can gain a more comprehensive view of network activity and detect incidents that might be missed when analyzing individual data sources.

User and entity behavior analytics (UEBA) is another technique that organizations use to identify security incidents.

This method focuses on monitoring the behavior of users and entities within the network to identify deviations from normal patterns.

For example, UEBA can detect when a user accesses resources they don't typically use or when an entity exhibits unusual data access patterns.

Network-based detection methods, such as intrusion detection and prevention systems (IDPS), are also widely used to identify security incidents.

These systems analyze network traffic and packets to identify known attack signatures, malicious payloads, or unusual network behavior.

They can be effective at detecting various types of network-based attacks, such as distributed denial-of-service (DDoS) attacks, port scans, and malware communications.

Another critical method for identifying security incidents is through the analysis of security intelligence feeds and threat intelligence.

These feeds provide organizations with information about emerging threats, known attack techniques, and indicators of compromise (IoCs) that can be used to identify incidents.

By continuously monitoring these feeds and comparing them to network and system data, organizations can quickly identify incidents related to known threats.

Furthermore, organizations may employ the use of honeypots and decoy systems as a proactive method for identifying security incidents.

Honeypots are intentionally vulnerable systems that are set up to attract attackers.

When an attacker interacts with a honeypot, it can trigger alerts and provide valuable insights into the attacker's tactics and tools, helping to identify security incidents in progress.

Additionally, organizations can utilize file and malware analysis tools to identify security incidents related to malicious files or software.

These tools analyze the characteristics of files and executables to detect malicious code or behaviors, helping organizations identify malware infections or suspicious files on their systems.

In some cases, organizations also use network forensics and packet capture tools to identify security incidents.

These tools capture and analyze network traffic at a granular level, allowing security teams to reconstruct and investigate incidents, even after they have occurred.

Network forensics can help identify the source of a security incident, the methods used by attackers, and the extent of the compromise.

Furthermore, threat hunting is a proactive method used by organizations to identify security incidents that may have gone unnoticed by automated detection systems.

Security analysts actively search for signs of compromise within the network by analyzing data, logs, and network traffic to identify abnormal or suspicious behavior.

Collaboration with external organizations, such as threat intelligence sharing groups and information security communities, can also assist in identifying security incidents.

These external sources may provide information about emerging threats and vulnerabilities that can help organizations detect and respond to incidents.

In summary, organizations employ a range of methods and techniques to identify security incidents, including continuous monitoring, intrusion detection systems, endpoint detection and response, security event correlation, user and entity behavior analytics, network-based detection, security intelligence feeds, honeypots, file and malware analysis, network forensics, threat hunting, and collaboration with external organizations.

By leveraging these methods and techniques, organizations can enhance their ability to detect and respond to security incidents effectively, ultimately minimizing the impact of cyber threats on their systems and data.

When it comes to managing security incidents, one of the critical steps in the incident response process is incident classification and severity assessment.

Incident classification involves categorizing incidents based on their nature, impact, and potential risks to the organization.

This classification helps incident response teams prioritize their actions and allocate resources effectively.

One common method for incident classification is to use a tiered approach, categorizing incidents into different levels of severity.

These severity levels can range from low to critical, with each level indicating the level of potential harm and urgency of the incident.

Low-severity incidents typically have minimal impact and can be addressed with routine procedures.

Examples of low-severity incidents may include spam emails or minor malware infections that have not spread widely.

Medium-severity incidents are more significant in terms of potential impact but are not immediately critical.

These incidents may require a more in-depth investigation and response efforts, such as the containment and eradication of malware or a limited data breach.

High-severity incidents are those that have a substantial impact on the organization and require immediate attention.

Examples of high-severity incidents may include a widespread malware outbreak that disrupts critical systems or a data breach involving sensitive customer information.

Critical-severity incidents represent the most severe and urgent category.

These incidents pose an immediate and significant threat to the organization's operations, reputation, or data.

Examples of critical-severity incidents include a ransomware attack that has encrypted critical data or a network breach that exposes confidential information.

Incident classification helps incident response teams understand the potential consequences of an incident and guides their response efforts accordingly.

Severity assessment is closely related to incident classification, as it involves evaluating the specific impact and risks associated with an incident.

Severity assessment takes into account various factors, such as the potential loss of data, the disruption of critical systems, the financial impact, and the legal and regulatory implications.

To assess the severity of an incident accurately, incident response teams must consider both the immediate impact and the long-term consequences.

For example, a minor security incident that goes undetected and unaddressed may escalate into a more severe incident over time.

To assist in severity assessment, organizations often develop incident severity matrices or scoring systems.

These matrices assign numerical values or scores to different factors, such as the scope of the incident, the sensitivity of the data involved, and the potential financial impact.

By evaluating these factors and applying the matrix, incident response teams can determine the overall severity of the incident.

Severity assessment also considers the potential harm to the organization's reputation and customer trust.

A security incident that results in the exposure of sensitive customer information can lead to reputational damage and the loss of customer trust, which can have long-lasting consequences.

Additionally, severity assessment takes into account any legal and regulatory obligations that the organization must adhere to.

Certain incidents may trigger mandatory reporting requirements, which can result in legal and financial consequences if not addressed appropriately.

When assessing the severity of an incident, incident response teams should also consider the potential for data exfiltration or data manipulation.

Even if an incident initially appears to have a low impact, it may be more severe if it involves unauthorized access to critical systems or sensitive data.

As part of the severity assessment, incident response teams should engage with legal counsel to ensure compliance with relevant laws and regulations.

Moreover, severity assessment may involve consultation with external experts, such as cybersecurity consultants or forensic investigators, to evaluate the incident thoroughly.

Once the classification and severity assessment are complete, incident response teams can develop a tailored response strategy.

High-severity incidents typically require a swift and comprehensive response, including immediate containment and eradication measures.

Medium-severity incidents may involve a more focused response effort, while low-severity incidents can often be managed with routine procedures.

It's crucial for incident response teams to communicate the severity of the incident to key stakeholders within the organization, including senior management, legal counsel, and IT teams.

Clear and timely communication ensures that everyone understands the urgency of the situation and can collaborate effectively to mitigate the incident's impact.

In summary, incident classification and severity assessment are essential steps in the incident response process.

These processes help incident response teams prioritize their actions, allocate resources effectively, and determine the appropriate response strategy.

By accurately classifying incidents and assessing their severity, organizations can respond to security incidents in a manner that minimizes the impact and potential harm to the organization's operations, reputation, and data.

Chapter 4: Building an Incident Response Team

In the realm of cybersecurity, forming an effective incident response team is a fundamental step in safeguarding an organization's assets and data.

This team is a critical component of an organization's defense against cyber threats, as it plays a pivotal role in detecting, responding to, and mitigating security incidents.

The composition of an incident response team varies depending on the organization's size, industry, and specific needs.

However, there are common roles and responsibilities that should be considered when forming such a team.

First and foremost, the incident response team should have a designated incident commander, a leader who oversees and coordinates all response efforts.

The incident commander is responsible for making critical decisions, managing resources, and ensuring that the incident response plan is executed effectively.

Additionally, the incident commander serves as the primary point of contact for senior management and external stakeholders.

Another crucial role within the incident response team is the technical analyst, an individual responsible for investigating and analyzing security incidents.

These analysts possess deep technical expertise and play a vital role in understanding the nature and scope of the incident.

Their responsibilities include identifying the root cause of the incident, assessing its impact, and gathering evidence for further analysis.

Legal counsel is another key member of the incident response team, providing guidance on legal and regulatory matters throughout the response process.

Legal experts ensure that the organization complies with relevant laws and regulations, especially when dealing with incidents that involve sensitive data or potential legal ramifications.

Moreover, the incident response team includes communication coordinators who manage communication both within the organization and with external entities.

These individuals are responsible for keeping stakeholders informed, providing updates on the incident's progress, and maintaining transparency throughout the response effort.

Clear and timely communication is crucial in managing the incident effectively and maintaining trust with employees, customers, and partners.

A critical role within the incident response team is the forensics expert, someone with expertise in digital forensics and evidence preservation.

Forensics experts play a vital role in collecting and analyzing digital evidence related to the incident.

They ensure that evidence is handled and preserved in a manner that adheres to legal standards and can be used in potential legal proceedings.

In some cases, the incident response team may also include public relations or media relations specialists.

These individuals manage the organization's public image and reputation during and after a security incident.

They help craft messaging to address the incident with stakeholders, customers, and the media, ensuring that the organization's reputation is managed effectively.

Moreover, external liaisons can be part of the incident response team, connecting the organization with law enforcement agencies, regulatory bodies, and industry groups.

These liaisons facilitate cooperation, information sharing, and coordination with external entities, especially when the incident involves criminal activity or regulatory requirements.

The incident response team should also have access to subject matter experts (SMEs) who can provide specialized knowledge in areas such as malware analysis, network forensics, or cloud security.

These experts can be consulted as needed to address specific aspects of the incident that require specialized expertise.

Assembling an effective incident response team requires careful consideration of the individuals' skills, expertise, and availability.

Cross-functional teams that include representatives from various departments, including IT, legal, communications, and security, are often the most effective in addressing security incidents comprehensively.

Furthermore, the incident response team should have a clear understanding of the organization's incident response plan and its specific roles and responsibilities within that plan.

Regular training and tabletop exercises can help ensure that team members are well-prepared to respond to incidents effectively.

In summary, forming an effective incident response team is a critical step in an organization's cybersecurity strategy.

The team's composition, roles, and responsibilities should be tailored to the organization's unique needs and should encompass technical expertise, legal guidance, communication skills, and specialized knowledge.

By having a well-structured and trained incident response team in place, organizations can enhance their ability to detect, respond to, and mitigate security incidents effectively, ultimately minimizing the impact of cyber threats.

When it comes to managing security incidents, the roles and responsibilities within the incident response team are crucial for ensuring a coordinated and effective response.
Each member of the team has specific duties that contribute to the overall goal of detecting, mitigating, and recovering from security incidents.
Let's delve into these roles and responsibilities to gain a better understanding of how an incident response team operates.

Incident Commander: The incident commander is the leader of the response effort. This individual is responsible for making critical decisions, coordinating the team's activities, and ensuring that the incident response plan is executed effectively. The incident commander also serves as the primary point of contact for senior management and external stakeholders, providing them with updates on the incident's progress.

Technical Analysts: Technical analysts play a pivotal role in investigating and analyzing security incidents. They have deep technical expertise and are responsible for identifying the root cause of the incident, assessing its impact, and gathering evidence for further analysis. These analysts use their technical skills to understand the nature and scope of the incident, enabling the team to respond appropriately.

Legal Counsel: Legal experts within the incident response team provide guidance on legal and regulatory matters throughout the response process. They ensure that the organization complies with relevant laws and regulations, especially when dealing with incidents involving sensitive data or potential legal ramifications. Legal counsel helps the organization navigate complex legal issues that may arise during the response.

Communication Coordinators: Communication coordinators are responsible for managing both internal and external communication during the incident response. They keep stakeholders informed, provide updates on the incident's progress, and maintain transparency throughout the response effort. Clear and timely communication is essential for managing the incident effectively and maintaining trust with employees, customers, and partners.

Forensics Experts: Forensics experts specialize in digital forensics and evidence preservation. They play a critical role in collecting and analyzing digital evidence related to the incident. These experts ensure that evidence is handled and preserved in a manner that adheres to legal standards and can be used in potential legal proceedings. Their work is instrumental in understanding the full scope of the incident.

Public Relations/Media Relations Specialists: In some cases, public relations or media relations specialists are part of the incident response team. These individuals manage the organization's public image and reputation during and after a security incident. They help craft messaging to address the incident with stakeholders, customers, and the media, ensuring that the organization's reputation is managed effectively.

External Liaisons: External liaisons connect the organization with law enforcement agencies, regulatory bodies, and industry groups. They facilitate cooperation, information sharing, and coordination with external entities, especially when the incident involves criminal activity or regulatory requirements. Building and maintaining relationships with external partners are crucial for a successful response.

Subject Matter Experts (SMEs): SMEs provide specialized knowledge in specific areas, such as malware analysis, network forensics, or cloud security. They can be consulted as needed to address specific aspects of the incident that require specialized expertise. SMEs bring in-depth knowledge to the team and help ensure that all facets of the incident are thoroughly investigated and understood.

Cross-Functional Teams: Cross-functional teams that include representatives from various departments, including IT, legal, communications, and security, are often the most effective in addressing security incidents comprehensively. Collaboration across different functions ensures that the incident response team has a diverse range of expertise and can tackle multifaceted challenges.

Training and Preparedness: Regardless of their specific roles, all members of the incident response team should have a clear understanding of the organization's incident response plan and their roles within it. Regular training and tabletop exercises help ensure that team members are well-prepared to respond to incidents effectively.

Compliance and Regulatory Experts: In cases where security incidents may have compliance and regulatory implications, experts in this area play a vital role. They ensure that the organization follows relevant regulations and reporting requirements, helping to mitigate potential legal consequences.

Security Operations Center (SOC) Analysts: In organizations with dedicated Security Operations Centers, SOC analysts may be involved in monitoring, detecting, and escalating security incidents in real time. Their role is crucial in identifying potential threats early and initiating the incident response process promptly.

In summary, the roles and responsibilities within the incident response team are diverse and multifaceted. Each member brings unique skills and expertise to the table, contributing to the team's ability to respond effectively to security incidents. Collaboration, clear communication, and a well-defined incident response plan are essential elements of a successful incident response team.

Chapter 5: Incident Triage and Prioritization

When it comes to incident response, one of the crucial steps in effectively managing security incidents is the triage process.

Triage is a term borrowed from medical practice, where it refers to the process of determining the priority of patients' treatments based on the severity of their conditions.

In the context of incident response, triage involves assessing and prioritizing security incidents based on their potential impact and urgency.

The goal of the triage process is to ensure that limited resources are allocated to the most critical incidents first, allowing organizations to respond promptly and effectively.

Triage begins with the initial detection of a security incident, which can occur through various means, such as intrusion detection systems, security monitoring tools, or user reports.

Once an incident is detected, it is essential to promptly initiate the triage process to assess the situation accurately.

The first step in triage is to gather essential information about the incident.

This includes identifying the affected systems, understanding the nature of the incident, and determining the potential impact on the organization.

Information gathering may involve reviewing log files, analyzing network traffic, and interviewing individuals who reported the incident or were involved in its detection.

Effective communication within the incident response team is critical during this phase to ensure that all relevant details are collected.

After gathering initial information, the next step in triage is to classify the incident.

Incidents are categorized based on their nature and impact, using predefined incident classification criteria.

Common incident categories may include malware infections, unauthorized access attempts, data breaches, and denial-of-service attacks.

Each category may have predefined severity levels that help prioritize incidents.

For example, a data breach involving sensitive customer information is typically classified as a high-severity incident due to its potential impact on the organization and its customers.

Once the incident is classified, it is essential to assess its severity accurately.

Severity assessment involves evaluating the potential harm and risks associated with the incident.

Factors considered during severity assessment may include the scope of the incident, the sensitivity of the data involved, the potential financial impact, and the legal and regulatory implications.

It is crucial to assess both the immediate impact and the long-term consequences of the incident.

For instance, a malware infection that appears minor initially may have a more severe impact if it spreads to critical systems or if it leads to data exfiltration.

Severity assessment often involves using predefined scoring systems or matrices that assign numerical values to various incident attributes.

These matrices help incident responders objectively evaluate the incident's severity and prioritize their response efforts accordingly.

In addition to assessing the technical aspects of the incident, triage should consider the broader context, including the organization's critical assets and the potential for reputational damage.

For example, an incident that involves the compromise of intellectual property or trade secrets may be considered severe, even if the technical impact appears limited.

Once the incident's severity is assessed, the incident response team can determine the appropriate response actions.

High-severity incidents typically require a swift and comprehensive response, including immediate containment and eradication measures.

For example, if a critical system is compromised by malware, isolating the affected system from the network and initiating malware removal procedures are top priorities.

Medium-severity incidents may involve a more focused response effort, such as investigating the incident, identifying the root cause, and implementing corrective actions.

Low-severity incidents may be addressed with routine procedures, such as resetting user passwords or cleaning up minor malware infections.

Throughout the triage process, clear communication is essential.

Effective communication ensures that all team members are informed of the incident's status, severity, and the actions being taken.

It also allows for timely reporting to senior management and external stakeholders, especially in high-severity incidents that may have broader implications.

Furthermore, incident documentation is a critical aspect of the triage process.

Accurate and detailed documentation of the incident, including the actions taken and the lessons learned, is essential for post-incident analysis and reporting.

Documentation also helps organizations improve their incident response processes over time.

Finally, it is worth noting that the triage process is not static.

As new information becomes available and the incident evolves, the assessment of severity and response actions may need to be adjusted accordingly.

Flexibility and adaptability are key attributes of effective triage and incident response.

In summary, the triage process is a vital component of incident response, helping organizations prioritize and respond to security incidents effectively.

By gathering information, classifying incidents, assessing severity, and taking appropriate actions, incident response teams can mitigate the impact of security incidents and protect the organization's assets and reputation.

Prioritizing security incidents based on their impact and risk is a critical aspect of effective incident response.

It involves making informed decisions about which incidents to address first and allocating resources accordingly.

To prioritize incidents effectively, it's essential to understand the concept of impact and risk in the context of cybersecurity.

Impact refers to the consequences or harm that a security incident can inflict on an organization.

It encompasses both immediate and long-term effects, including financial losses, damage to the organization's reputation, regulatory fines, and operational disruptions.

Understanding the potential impact of an incident is crucial because it helps incident responders gauge the severity of the situation and determine the appropriate response.

Risk, on the other hand, involves assessing the likelihood of a security incident occurring and its potential consequences.

It considers factors such as vulnerabilities in the organization's systems, the effectiveness of existing security controls, and the threat landscape.

Risk assessment helps organizations prioritize incidents by identifying those with a higher likelihood of occurrence and significant potential impact.

When prioritizing incidents, it's essential to have a structured approach that takes into account both impact and risk.

One commonly used method is to create an incident prioritization matrix.

This matrix assigns numerical values to the severity of impact and the likelihood of occurrence, and then calculates a risk score for each incident.

Incidents with higher risk scores are given higher priority.

However, the specific criteria and scoring system used may vary depending on the organization's needs and industry regulations.

In addition to the severity of impact and likelihood of occurrence, there are other factors that may influence incident prioritization.

One such factor is the criticality of the affected systems or assets.

Incidents that threaten critical systems or sensitive data are typically given higher priority because of their potential to cause significant harm.

Another factor to consider is the potential for legal or regulatory consequences.

Incidents that may lead to non-compliance with data protection laws, privacy regulations, or industry standards often require immediate attention to mitigate legal and financial risks.

The timing of incident detection can also impact prioritization.

Incidents that are detected promptly and responded to quickly are more likely to be contained before they escalate, reducing their overall impact.

Conversely, incidents that go undetected for an extended period may require a more intensive response effort.

Additionally, the persistence of an attacker can influence prioritization.

If an attacker continues to exploit a vulnerability or maintain unauthorized access, the incident may escalate in severity, warranting a higher priority response.

Resource availability is another consideration when prioritizing incidents.

Organizations may have limited resources, such as incident responders, forensic analysts, or legal counsel.

Efforts should be focused on incidents where resources can be most effectively applied to minimize impact and risk.

To illustrate the prioritization process, consider an example involving two security incidents:

Incident A involves a minor malware infection on a non-critical user's computer.

Incident B involves a data breach in which customer data, including financial information, may have been exposed.

While Incident A may have a low impact on the organization, Incident B has the potential for significant financial and reputational damage, making it a higher-priority incident.

The incident response team would allocate resources and respond to Incident B with greater urgency to mitigate its impact and address the associated risks.

It's important to note that incident prioritization is not a one-time decision but an ongoing process.

As new information becomes available or the incident evolves, the priority may need to be reassessed and adjusted.

Effective communication within the incident response team is essential during this process to ensure that all members are aligned on the prioritization decisions.

In summary, prioritizing security incidents based on impact and risk is a crucial aspect of incident response.

By assessing the potential consequences of an incident, its likelihood of occurrence, and other relevant factors, organizations can allocate resources effectively and focus their efforts on addressing the most critical threats.

A structured and adaptable approach to prioritization helps organizations minimize the impact of security incidents and safeguard their assets and reputation.

Chapter 6: Investigating Security Incidents

Gathering and analyzing evidence is a fundamental aspect of incident response and digital forensics.

It involves collecting, preserving, and examining digital artifacts to understand the nature of a security incident, identify the responsible parties, and support legal or disciplinary actions if necessary.

The process of gathering and analyzing evidence is meticulous and requires a systematic approach to ensure the integrity and admissibility of the collected data.

The first step in this process is to establish a chain of custody for all collected evidence.

A chain of custody is a documented record that tracks the handling and custody of evidence from the moment it is collected until it is presented in court or used for internal purposes.

Maintaining a clear chain of custody is critical to ensure that the evidence is admissible in legal proceedings and has not been tampered with or compromised.

Once the chain of custody is established, the evidence collection phase begins.

This phase involves identifying and securing all relevant digital artifacts, such as files, logs, system memory, and network traffic.

Evidence may reside on various types of devices, including computers, servers, mobile devices, and network appliances.

To collect evidence effectively, incident responders and forensic analysts must follow established procedures and use specialized tools and techniques.

Forensic imaging tools, for example, create exact copies (bit-for-bit) of storage devices, preserving the original data while allowing analysts to work with duplicates, reducing the risk of altering the original evidence.

Additionally, volatile data, such as information stored in system memory, must be collected and preserved before it is lost when a system is powered down.

Once evidence is collected, it must be carefully documented, cataloged, and labeled to maintain the chain of custody.

Each piece of evidence should be assigned a unique identifier, and detailed records should be kept to track its handling, storage, and access.

Proper documentation is crucial for demonstrating the integrity of the evidence and ensuring its admissibility in court. After evidence collection is complete, the analysis phase begins. During this phase, forensic analysts examine the collected evidence to answer specific questions related to the incident. The analysis may involve a wide range of activities, depending on the nature of the incident.

For example, if the incident involves a malware infection, analysts may examine malware samples to understand their functionality and origin. If the incident pertains to unauthorized access, analysts may analyze log files and network traffic to identify the attacker's entry point and actions. Throughout the analysis, forensic analysts adhere to established guidelines and best practices to maintain the integrity of the evidence.

They use specialized forensic tools and techniques to recover deleted files, uncover hidden data, and identify signs of tampering or manipulation.

In some cases, evidence may need to be decrypted or decoded to reveal its contents fully.

Moreover, analysts use various hashing algorithms to verify the integrity of evidence and ensure that it has not been altered during the analysis process.

Throughout the analysis, analysts maintain a detailed record of their findings, documenting their methodologies, observations, and conclusions.

This documentation is critical for creating a clear and comprehensive report that summarizes the results of the analysis.

A well-prepared forensic report can be used in legal proceedings, internal investigations, or as a reference for incident response efforts.

In addition to technical analysis, forensic analysts may also be involved in providing expert testimony in court cases.

Their expertise and ability to present their findings in a clear and understandable manner are essential for assisting judges and juries in understanding complex technical details.

Furthermore, forensic analysts must adhere to ethical and legal standards throughout the evidence-gathering and analysis process.

This includes respecting individuals' privacy rights, following applicable laws and regulations, and ensuring that evidence is collected legally and ethically.

In cases involving employee misconduct, for example, organizations must balance their need to investigate with respecting employees' rights.

Finally, organizations should consider the long-term storage and retention of evidence.

Digital evidence, like any other type of evidence, may need to be retained for an extended period, especially if it is related to legal or regulatory matters.

Organizations should have clear policies and procedures for evidence retention and disposal to ensure compliance with legal requirements.

In summary, gathering and analyzing evidence is a crucial component of incident response and digital forensics.

It involves collecting, preserving, and examining digital artifacts to understand security incidents, identify responsible parties, and support legal or disciplinary actions.

Maintaining a clear chain of custody, following established procedures, and adhering to ethical and legal standards are essential aspects of effective evidence management.

Forensic analysts play a critical role in ensuring the integrity of evidence and providing valuable insights into security incidents. Digital forensics plays a crucial role in incident investigation by helping organizations uncover and analyze digital evidence related to security incidents.

It involves the systematic examination of digital devices, systems, and data to gather information, identify the cause of incidents, and support legal or disciplinary actions if necessary.

Incident investigation often begins with the identification of a security incident, which can include a wide range of events, such as data breaches, malware infections, insider threats, and network intrusions.

Once an incident is detected or suspected, organizations initiate an investigation to determine its scope, impact, and the extent of any compromise.

Digital forensics specialists are instrumental in this process, as they possess the expertise to collect and analyze digital evidence that can shed light on the incident's origins and implications.

The first step in digital forensics investigation is to identify and secure the relevant digital devices and data sources.

This may involve seizing servers, computers, mobile devices, network logs, and any other potential sources of evidence.

It is essential to follow established protocols and maintain a clear chain of custody to preserve the integrity and admissibility of the evidence.

Once evidence is secured, forensic specialists employ various tools and techniques to analyze it.

This analysis may include examining file systems, registry entries, memory dumps, network traffic, and application logs to reconstruct the sequence of events leading up to and during the incident.

One of the key goals of digital forensics in incident investigation is to determine the extent of the compromise and assess the impact on the organization.

For example, in the case of a data breach, digital forensics can help identify which data was accessed, how it was exfiltrated, and who was responsible.

In the event of a malware infection, forensic analysis can reveal the malware's functionality, propagation methods, and potential damage.

Throughout the investigation, forensic specialists maintain detailed records of their findings, including the steps taken, tools used, and the evidence examined.

This documentation is essential for producing comprehensive reports that summarize the results of the investigation and provide a clear account of the incident's details. Moreover, digital forensics is often employed to attribute the incident to specific individuals or groups.

By analyzing digital evidence, investigators can trace the actions of threat actors, such as hackers or insiders, and build a case against them.

Attribution can be challenging, as sophisticated attackers often take measures to hide their tracks, but digital forensics experts use their skills to uncover clues and establish links between evidence and potential culprits.

In some cases, digital forensics may lead to legal actions, such as criminal prosecutions or civil litigation.

Forensic specialists may be called upon to provide expert testimony in court, explaining their findings and the significance of digital evidence to judges and juries.

Expert testimony can be critical in helping legal proceedings understand complex technical details and make informed decisions. Moreover, digital forensics in incident investigation helps organizations improve their security posture by identifying vulnerabilities and weaknesses that led to the incident.

By understanding how an incident occurred, organizations can take steps to prevent similar incidents in the future, enhance security controls, and implement better incident response strategies.

Digital forensics also plays a role in ensuring compliance with various regulations and standards.

Many industries and jurisdictions have specific requirements for data protection, breach notification, and incident reporting.

Digital evidence gathered during an investigation can be used to demonstrate compliance with these requirements.

Finally, digital forensics is an ever-evolving field, as technology and threat landscapes continually change.

Forensic specialists must stay current with the latest tools and techniques to remain effective in their roles.

They often engage in ongoing training and professional development to ensure they have the skills and knowledge necessary to handle complex investigations.

In summary, digital forensics is a critical component of incident investigation, enabling organizations to uncover, analyze, and attribute security incidents. It plays a vital role in understanding the scope and impact of incidents, supporting legal actions, improving security, ensuring compliance, and advancing the field of cybersecurity.

Chapter 7: Containment and Eradication Strategies

Containment is a critical phase in managing a security incident, as it aims to prevent the incident from spreading further and causing additional harm to an organization's systems and data.

During this phase, incident responders must employ a set of strategies and tactics to isolate the affected systems, eliminate threats, and restore normal operations.

One of the first steps in containment is to identify the scope of the incident.

Incident responders need to determine how extensive the compromise is and which systems or assets have been affected.

This assessment helps in defining the boundaries for containment efforts.

Once the scope is understood, containment strategies can be tailored to address the specific incident.

A common approach is to isolate compromised systems from the network to prevent attackers from accessing or exfiltrating data.

This can be achieved by disconnecting affected devices from the network or by implementing network segmentation to contain the incident within a limited area.

In addition to network isolation, incident responders may choose to isolate affected systems physically by removing them from the network entirely.

For example, if a server is compromised, it may be taken offline to prevent further unauthorized access.

Isolation measures must be carefully planned and executed to minimize disruptions to normal business operations.

Containment efforts should also include identifying and closing vulnerabilities or security weaknesses that allowed the incident to occur in the first place.

This may involve patching or updating software, changing configurations, or strengthening access controls.

For instance, if the incident resulted from a known software vulnerability, patching that vulnerability on affected systems can prevent similar incidents from occurring.

Another crucial aspect of containment is removing malicious software or artifacts from compromised systems.

This process is known as remediation and involves eliminating malware, backdoors, or other unauthorized code.

It can be a complex and time-consuming task, as attackers often use sophisticated techniques to maintain persistence on compromised systems.

Remediation may also include cleaning up compromised accounts and resetting passwords to prevent unauthorized access.

In some cases, organizations may choose to rebuild affected systems entirely to ensure they are free of any lingering threats.

Throughout the containment phase, organizations should closely monitor the affected systems to ensure that containment measures remain effective.

Continuous monitoring helps detect any attempts by attackers to regain access or escalate their privileges.

It is essential to remain vigilant and adapt containment strategies as needed to stay ahead of the threat.

Furthermore, communication is crucial during containment efforts.

All relevant stakeholders, including senior management, legal teams, and public relations, should be informed about the incident and containment progress.

Effective communication helps manage expectations and keeps everyone aligned on the organization's response efforts.

Additionally, containment strategies should consider the potential legal and regulatory implications of the incident.

Organizations may be required to report security incidents to regulatory authorities or notify affected individuals, depending on the nature and scope of the incident.

Containment efforts should align with these obligations to ensure compliance with data protection and breach notification laws.

Containment is not a one-size-fits-all process; it varies depending on the incident's nature and the organization's environment.

Some incidents may require immediate and aggressive containment measures, while others can be addressed more methodically.

The ultimate goal is to regain control over the affected systems, minimize damage, and prevent further compromise.

Once containment is successful, organizations can transition to the eradication and recovery phases of incident response, where they work to eliminate the root causes of the incident and restore normal operations.

In summary, strategies for containing a security incident are essential for preventing further harm and restoring control to an organization.

Containment efforts should be tailored to the incident's scope and nature, including isolating affected systems, closing vulnerabilities, removing malware, and closely monitoring the situation.

Effective communication and compliance with legal and regulatory requirements are also critical aspects of the containment process.

Eradication techniques and best practices are crucial components of the incident response process, as they focus on permanently removing threats and vulnerabilities from an organization's systems and network.

Once an incident has been contained, the next step is to eliminate the root causes and any lingering traces of the security breach.

Eradication efforts are designed to ensure that the incident does not recur and that the organization's environment is secure.

One of the primary eradications techniques is the removal of malicious software or artifacts that may have been introduced during the incident.

This includes identifying and deleting malware, trojans, rootkits, or any other unauthorized code that may have been installed on compromised systems.

Eradication also involves identifying and addressing vulnerabilities or weaknesses that allowed the incident to occur.

For example, if the incident was a result of an unpatched software vulnerability, applying the necessary patches or updates to affected systems is a crucial eradication step.

Similarly, configuration changes may be necessary to prevent attackers from exploiting known weaknesses.

During the eradication phase, organizations should also review and strengthen access controls.

This may involve revoking unauthorized access, resetting passwords, and reconfiguring permissions to ensure that only authorized users have access to systems and data.

Additionally, organizations should conduct a thorough review of user accounts and privileges to identify any suspicious or unauthorized accounts created by the attackers.

Removing these accounts and restricting privileges to the minimum necessary can help prevent future incidents.

It's important to keep in mind that eradicating threats may not be a straightforward process, especially if the attackers used advanced or persistent techniques to maintain access.

In such cases, organizations may need to engage in a more extensive and methodical eradication effort.

This may involve rebuilding compromised systems from scratch to ensure that no hidden backdoors or artifacts remain.

Furthermore, organizations should consider the broader impact of the incident and evaluate whether any data or systems were compromised.

If sensitive data was exposed, organizations must follow data breach notification requirements and inform affected individuals or regulatory authorities as necessary.

As with other phases of incident response, communication is key during the eradication phase.

Stakeholders, including senior management, legal teams, and IT staff, should be kept informed about the progress of eradication efforts.

Clear and timely communication helps manage expectations and ensures that everyone is aligned on the organization's response.

In some cases, organizations may choose to engage external experts, such as digital forensics specialists or incident response consultants, to assist with eradication efforts.

These experts bring specialized knowledge and tools that can be instrumental in thorough threat removal and system hardening.

While eradicating threats is a critical step in incident response, it's important to remember that the process does not end with eradication.

After successfully removing threats and vulnerabilities, organizations should transition to the recovery phase, where they work to restore normal operations and ensure that systems are secure.

This includes verifying that all necessary patches and updates have been applied, reviewing security configurations, and conducting comprehensive testing to confirm that the organization's environment is resilient against future attacks.

In summary, eradication techniques and best practices are essential for ensuring that security incidents are fully addressed and do not recur.

Eradication efforts involve removing malicious software, addressing vulnerabilities, and strengthening access controls.

Thorough communication and, if necessary, external expertise can enhance the effectiveness of eradication efforts.

Ultimately, the goal is to eliminate threats and secure the organization's systems and network for the future.

Chapter 8: Recovery and Lessons Learned

Post-incident recovery planning is a critical phase in the incident response process that focuses on restoring normal operations after a security incident.

While containment and eradication efforts aim to stop the incident and eliminate its root causes, recovery planning ensures that an organization can bounce back and resume its regular activities.

Recovery planning involves several key steps, including assessing the impact of the incident, prioritizing recovery efforts, and developing a comprehensive recovery plan.

One of the first tasks in post-incident recovery planning is to conduct a thorough assessment of the incident's impact.

This assessment helps organizations understand the extent of the damage, including the systems and data affected, the duration of the incident, and the potential financial and reputational consequences.

It's essential to involve key stakeholders, such as IT teams, legal counsel, and senior management, in this assessment to ensure a comprehensive understanding of the situation.

Once the impact assessment is complete, organizations can prioritize their recovery efforts.

Not all systems and data may be equally critical to the organization's operations, so it's crucial to identify the most important assets and services that need to be restored first.

This prioritization ensures that limited resources are allocated to the most critical areas, allowing the organization to recover quickly.

In addition to prioritizing recovery efforts, organizations should also consider the order in which systems and services should be restored.

Some systems may need to be brought back online before others to minimize disruption to business operations.

For example, email and communication systems may be a top priority to ensure that employees can communicate and collaborate effectively during the recovery process.

Once the priorities are established, organizations can begin developing a recovery plan.

The recovery plan outlines the specific steps, tasks, and resources required to restore systems and services.

It includes details on who is responsible for each task, the timeline for completion, and any dependencies between tasks.

The plan should also specify the criteria for declaring the recovery process successful and the conditions under which normal operations can resume.

In some cases, organizations may choose to create separate recovery plans for different types of incidents, such as data breaches, malware infections, or network outages.

These plans can be tailored to the unique challenges and requirements associated with each incident type.

During the recovery planning process, organizations should also consider the legal and regulatory implications of the incident.

Depending on the nature of the incident and the industry in which the organization operates, there may be reporting requirements or obligations to notify affected individuals or regulatory authorities.

Ensuring compliance with these obligations is an essential aspect of post-incident recovery.

Recovery planning should also address communication and public relations strategies.

Organizations should be prepared to communicate with customers, partners, employees, and other stakeholders about the incident and the recovery process.

Effective communication helps manage expectations, build trust, and minimize the reputational damage that can result from a security incident.

Furthermore, organizations should test their recovery plans through tabletop exercises or simulations.

These exercises help identify any weaknesses or gaps in the plan and allow teams to practice their roles and responsibilities in a controlled environment.

Regular testing and refinement of recovery plans ensure that organizations are well-prepared to execute them effectively when a real incident occurs.

Another important consideration in post-incident recovery planning is resource allocation.

Organizations should have a clear understanding of the resources required for recovery, including personnel, equipment, and third-party services.

Having access to the necessary resources ensures that the recovery process can proceed smoothly and without unnecessary delays.

Finally, recovery planning should incorporate lessons learned from the incident.

After the incident is resolved, organizations should conduct a post-incident review to assess the response efforts and identify areas for improvement.

This feedback loop helps organizations refine their incident response processes and enhance their overall cybersecurity posture.

In summary, post-incident recovery planning is a critical phase in the incident response process that focuses on restoring normal operations after a security incident.

It involves assessing the impact of the incident, prioritizing recovery efforts, developing a recovery plan, and considering legal, regulatory, and communication aspects.

Regular testing and learning from past incidents contribute to a more effective recovery process and better resilience against future threats.

Conducting a post-incident review is an essential step in the incident response process, as it allows organizations to reflect on their response efforts and learn from their experiences.

A post-incident review, also known as a post-mortem or lessons learned session, provides an opportunity for incident response teams to assess what went well during the response and where there is room for improvement.

The primary goal of a post-incident review is to identify strengths and weaknesses in the organization's incident response process, ultimately leading to more effective and efficient responses in the future.

To conduct a post-incident review effectively, organizations should assemble a cross-functional team that includes representatives from IT, security, legal, and other relevant departments.

Having a diverse set of perspectives helps ensure that all aspects of the incident response are considered.

The first step in the review process is to gather all available information related to the incident.

This includes incident reports, logs, communication records, and any documentation created during the response.

Having a comprehensive dataset is essential for a thorough analysis.

Once the data is collected, the team can begin the analysis phase.

This involves examining the timeline of events leading up to and during the incident.

The team should identify key milestones, actions taken, and decisions made during the response.

It's important to focus not only on the technical aspects of the incident but also on the organizational and communication aspects.

For example, the team should assess how well communication flowed within the response team and with external stakeholders.

Identifying bottlenecks or breakdowns in communication is crucial for improving incident response processes.

During the analysis phase, the team should also review the incident's impact on the organization.

This includes quantifying financial losses, operational disruptions, and reputational damage.

Understanding the full extent of the incident's impact helps organizations prioritize improvements in their response capabilities.

In addition to assessing what went well, the team should identify areas where the response could have been more effective.

This may include shortcomings in detection and alerting, delays in containment, or challenges in coordinating the response efforts.

The goal is not to assign blame but to identify opportunities for improvement.

After identifying strengths and weaknesses, the team should work together to develop actionable recommendations for enhancing the incident response process.

These recommendations should be specific, measurable, and focused on addressing the identified weaknesses.

For example, if the analysis reveals that detection capabilities were insufficient, a recommendation might be to invest in improved threat detection technology or enhance threat hunting practices.

Once the recommendations are formulated, organizations should prioritize them based on their potential impact and feasibility.

Some recommendations may require significant resources or changes in processes, while others may be relatively easy to implement.

Prioritization helps organizations make informed decisions about where to allocate their resources for improvement.

It's important to involve key stakeholders, including senior management, in the decision-making process to ensure that there is buy-in and support for the proposed changes.

After prioritization, organizations can create an action plan for implementing the recommendations.

This plan should outline the steps, responsibilities, and timelines for each improvement initiative.

Having a well-defined action plan helps organizations track progress and hold accountable those responsible for implementing the changes.

Regular monitoring and reporting on the progress of the action plan are essential to ensure that improvements are on track.

In addition to implementing recommended changes, organizations should consider conducting tabletop exercises or simulations to test their improved incident response processes.

These exercises help teams practice their roles and responsibilities in a controlled environment, making them better prepared for real incidents.

Finally, it's crucial to document the outcomes of the post-incident review and the actions taken in response to it.

This documentation serves as a valuable resource for future incident response efforts and provides a record of how the organization continually improves its security posture.

In summary, conducting a post-incident review and learning from incidents are critical aspects of an effective incident response process.

These activities help organizations assess their response efforts, identify strengths and weaknesses, and develop actionable recommendations for improvement.

By prioritizing and implementing these recommendations, organizations can enhance their incident response capabilities and better protect their assets and data from future threats.

Chapter 9: Automation and Incident Response

The role of automation in incident response is becoming increasingly significant in the ever-evolving landscape of cybersecurity.

Automation refers to the use of technology and predefined processes to perform tasks without human intervention.

In the context of incident response, automation plays a crucial role in accelerating response times, improving consistency, and reducing the manual workload on cybersecurity teams.

One of the key benefits of automation in incident response is its ability to speed up detection and alerting.

Cyber threats can evolve rapidly, and manual detection methods may not keep pace.

Automation can continuously monitor network traffic, logs, and security alerts, enabling organizations to identify potential incidents in real-time or even predict them before they occur.

Automated systems can analyze large volumes of data much faster than humans, allowing for the early detection of suspicious activities.

Once an incident is detected, automation can assist in the initial assessment and triage of the incident.

Automation tools can quickly gather additional information, such as affected systems, users, and potential indicators of compromise.

This information is essential for making informed decisions about the severity and impact of the incident.

Automated incident triage can also categorize incidents based on predefined criteria, helping incident response teams prioritize their efforts.

Automation can be particularly valuable in the containment phase of incident response.

When a security incident is confirmed, swift action is necessary to prevent further damage.

Automated responses can include isolating compromised systems from the network, blocking malicious IP addresses, or disabling compromised user accounts.

These actions can be executed rapidly and consistently, reducing the window of opportunity for attackers.

Furthermore, automation can facilitate the collection of digital evidence during an incident.

Digital forensics tools and scripts can be automated to preserve and analyze volatile data, system logs, and other critical artifacts.

This not only helps in understanding the scope of the incident but also ensures that evidence is properly preserved for potential legal or investigative purposes.

Another important role of automation is in the communication and notification process.

During an incident, it's crucial to keep stakeholders informed, including senior management, legal teams, and external parties.

Automation can generate and distribute incident reports, notifications, and updates, ensuring that everyone is well-informed about the incident's status and impact.

Furthermore, automation can assist in coordinating incident response efforts across different teams and departments within an organization.

Incident response workflows can be automated to assign tasks, track progress, and escalate issues when necessary.

This streamlines collaboration and ensures that everyone involved in the response is working cohesively.

Additionally, automation can play a role in the recovery phase of incident response.

Once an incident is contained and eradicated, systems and services need to be restored to normal operation.

Automation can assist in the deployment of updated configurations, patches, and security measures to prevent a recurrence of the incident.

Furthermore, automated testing can verify the integrity and security of systems before they are brought back online.

While automation offers numerous advantages in incident response, it is essential to acknowledge its limitations.

Not all aspects of incident response can be fully automated.

Human expertise and judgment are still crucial for decision-making, threat analysis, and complex investigations.

Furthermore, automation tools and processes need to be carefully designed and maintained to avoid introducing new vulnerabilities.

Automated responses should be regularly tested and validated to ensure they function as intended and do not inadvertently disrupt legitimate operations.

It's also important to consider the potential for false positives and false negatives when relying on automated detection and alerting systems.

To maximize the benefits of automation in incident response, organizations should adopt a holistic approach that combines automation with human expertise.

This approach, often referred to as "human-in-the-loop" or "augmented intelligence," leverages automation to handle repetitive and time-consuming tasks, allowing human analysts to focus on higher-level analysis and decision-making.

In summary, automation plays a vital role in incident response by accelerating detection, enhancing consistency, and reducing manual effort.

It can assist in detection, triage, containment, evidence collection, communication, coordination, and recovery.

However, automation should be complemented by human expertise to ensure effective decision-making and threat analysis.

Implementing automation tools and workflows in an organization's incident response process is a strategic move towards improving efficiency and reducing the manual burden on cybersecurity teams.

To successfully implement automation, it's essential to follow a well-defined plan and consider several key factors.

Firstly, organizations need to assess their current incident response processes and identify areas where automation can bring the most significant benefits.

This assessment should include an evaluation of the types of incidents the organization faces, the volume of alerts and events generated, and the existing technology stack.

By understanding the specific pain points and challenges, organizations can tailor their automation efforts to address their unique needs.

Once the areas for automation are identified, organizations should select suitable automation tools and technologies.

There is a wide range of automation solutions available, including Security Orchestration, Automation, and Response (SOAR) platforms, workflow automation tools, and scripting languages like Python.

The choice of tools depends on factors such as the organization's budget, technical expertise, and the complexity of the automation tasks.

It's crucial to select tools that can integrate seamlessly with existing security and IT systems, as this integration is key to the effectiveness of automation.

Integration ensures that automation workflows can access relevant data and trigger actions across the organization's technology stack.

When implementing automation, organizations should define clear objectives and goals.

What specific outcomes do they want to achieve through automation?

For example, objectives could include reducing incident response times, improving consistency in response actions, or minimizing the risk of human error.

Having well-defined objectives helps guide the automation implementation process and provides a basis for measuring its success.

Organizations should also establish metrics and key performance indicators (KPIs) to measure the impact of automation.

Metrics can include the time it takes to detect and respond to incidents, the number of incidents handled per unit of time, and the accuracy of automated responses.

These metrics help organizations assess the effectiveness of their automation efforts and make adjustments as needed.

Training and skill development are essential components of successful automation implementation.

Cybersecurity teams need the knowledge and skills to design, configure, and maintain automation workflows and tools.

Investing in training and development ensures that teams can maximize the benefits of automation and troubleshoot issues as they arise.

Furthermore, organizations should foster a culture of collaboration between cybersecurity teams and other departments, such as IT, legal, and compliance.

Automation often involves cross-functional workflows, and effective collaboration is crucial to ensure that automation aligns with the organization's overall objectives.

Clear communication and cooperation between teams also help identify opportunities for automation in areas beyond incident response.

Organizations should establish clear documentation and documentation practices for their automation workflows.

Documentation should include detailed descriptions of each workflow, including its purpose, inputs, outputs, and dependencies.

Comprehensive documentation ensures that automation processes can be understood and maintained over time, even if team members change.

It's important to regularly review and update documentation to reflect any changes or improvements to the automation workflows.

Security considerations are paramount in the implementation of automation tools and workflows.

Automation can introduce new risks if not properly secured.

Organizations should apply security best practices to automation solutions, including access controls, encryption, and regular vulnerability assessments.

Furthermore, organizations should monitor automation workflows for anomalies or unauthorized activities to detect and respond to potential security incidents.

Testing is a crucial phase in automation implementation.

Before deploying automation workflows in a production environment, organizations should thoroughly test them in a controlled environment.

Testing helps identify any issues or unexpected behaviors and allows for refinement and optimization of workflows.

It's also essential to have a rollback plan in case automation processes encounter unexpected problems in a production environment.

Continuous improvement is an ongoing effort in automation.

Organizations should regularly review the performance of their automation workflows and seek opportunities for optimization.

This may involve refining workflows, adding new automation tasks, or adjusting configurations based on the evolving threat landscape and organizational needs.

Feedback from cybersecurity teams and stakeholders is valuable in identifying areas for improvement.

In summary, implementing automation tools and workflows in incident response is a strategic move to enhance efficiency, consistency, and response times.

Organizations should assess their current processes, select suitable automation tools, define clear objectives, establish metrics, provide training, foster collaboration, document workflows, prioritize security, conduct thorough testing, and strive for continuous improvement.

Effective automation can significantly enhance an organization's ability to respond to security incidents and mitigate cyber threats effectively.

Chapter 10: Incident Response in the Modern Threat Landscape

In the dynamic landscape of cybersecurity, evolving threats and challenges continually test the resilience of organizations' security postures.

One of the most prominent challenges today is the rapid evolution of malware and malicious software.

Cybercriminals are constantly developing new and sophisticated forms of malware, including ransomware, Trojans, and spyware.

These malicious programs are designed to infiltrate systems, steal sensitive data, or disrupt operations, posing significant risks to organizations of all sizes.

Moreover, the rise of fileless malware, which operates in memory and leaves fewer traces, makes detection and mitigation even more challenging.

Phishing attacks continue to be a prevalent threat, with attackers using increasingly convincing and targeted tactics.

Phishing emails often impersonate trusted entities or individuals, tricking users into revealing sensitive information or downloading malicious payloads.

As organizations implement stronger email filtering and user awareness training, attackers adapt by refining their social engineering techniques.

Another evolving challenge is the growth of supply chain attacks.

Attackers are recognizing the value of targeting third-party suppliers and service providers as a means to compromise their intended targets.

Supply chain attacks can have far-reaching consequences, affecting multiple organizations connected to the compromised supplier.

Additionally, attacks on critical infrastructure, such as power grids, water treatment facilities, and transportation systems, pose a significant threat.

These attacks have the potential to disrupt essential services, causing widespread chaos and damage.

Nation-state-sponsored threats continue to evolve and become more sophisticated.

State-sponsored threat actors often have vast resources and advanced capabilities, enabling them to conduct cyber espionage, sabotage, and influence operations on a global scale.

Attributing these attacks to specific nations remains challenging, further complicating the response efforts.

The proliferation of the Internet of Things (IoT) introduces new challenges in terms of security.

IoT devices, ranging from smart thermostats to industrial sensors, often lack robust security measures, making them vulnerable to compromise.

When attackers breach IoT devices, they can gain access to networks and systems, potentially leading to data breaches or service disruptions.

As organizations embrace cloud computing and digital transformation, the attack surface expands.

Cloud environments offer numerous benefits, but they also introduce new security considerations.

Securing cloud resources, managing identity and access, and ensuring data privacy in the cloud require specialized skills and technologies.

Furthermore, insider threats remain a significant concern.

Malicious insiders or employees who inadvertently compromise security can pose a severe risk to organizations.

Detecting and mitigating insider threats require a combination of technical controls and monitoring, as well as an emphasis on fostering a positive security culture.

Cybersecurity professionals continually face the challenge of keeping pace with the evolving threat landscape.

Attackers are relentless in their pursuit of new vulnerabilities and attack vectors, which means that defenders must be equally vigilant.

Staying informed about emerging threats, vulnerabilities, and attack techniques is essential for effective defense.

Organizations also need to invest in advanced threat detection and response capabilities.

This includes the use of artificial intelligence (AI) and machine learning (ML) to analyze vast amounts of data for signs of suspicious activity.

Additionally, threat intelligence sharing and collaboration among organizations can help identify and respond to threats more effectively.

Legal and regulatory challenges are also on the rise in the cybersecurity landscape.

Data protection regulations, such as the General Data Protection Regulation (GDPR) and the California Consumer Privacy Act (CCPA), impose stringent requirements on organizations for the handling of personal data.

Non-compliance can result in significant fines and reputational damage.

Navigating the complex regulatory landscape while maintaining robust cybersecurity practices is a critical concern.

As organizations adopt new technologies, such as artificial intelligence, blockchain, and quantum computing, the security implications must be carefully considered.

These emerging technologies bring both opportunities and challenges, including the need to develop security measures that can adapt to evolving threats and exploit new capabilities.

In summary, the cybersecurity landscape is continually evolving, with threats and challenges becoming more sophisticated and diverse.

Organizations must remain proactive and agile in their approach to security, investing in advanced technologies, threat intelligence, and skilled personnel.

By staying informed, collaborating with others, and implementing robust security measures, organizations can better defend against the evolving threats of the digital age.

In the ever-evolving landscape of cybersecurity, adapting incident response strategies is imperative to effectively combat modern threats.

Traditional incident response approaches that once sufficed may no longer be adequate in addressing the sophisticated tactics employed by today's threat actors.

Modern threats often involve multifaceted and stealthy attacks that can bypass traditional security measures.

To adapt incident response strategies, organizations must first acknowledge the changing nature of cyber threats and the need for agility in their response efforts.

One significant shift in recent years is the move toward proactive threat hunting.

Rather than solely relying on alerts and reactive response, organizations are actively searching for signs of compromise within their networks.

Threat hunters use advanced analytics and threat intelligence to uncover hidden threats that may go undetected by automated security tools.

This proactive approach allows for faster detection and containment of threats.

Another essential aspect of modern incident response is the integration of threat intelligence.

Threat intelligence provides valuable context about current threats, including indicators of compromise, attack techniques, and threat actor behavior.

Integrating threat intelligence into incident response processes enables organizations to better understand the nature of the threats they face and respond more effectively.

Machine learning and artificial intelligence (AI) play a significant role in modern incident response.

These technologies can analyze vast amounts of data in real-time, identifying anomalies and potential threats that may have gone unnoticed by human analysts.

AI-driven tools can assist in threat detection, automated response, and even prediction of potential threats based on historical data.

Additionally, modern incident response strategies emphasize the importance of incident containment.

Traditional incident response often focused primarily on eradication and recovery, but containment has gained prominence due to the need to limit the damage caused by advanced threats.

Effective containment measures can prevent attackers from moving laterally within a network, thereby minimizing the scope of the incident.

Moreover, modern incident response incorporates the concept of "assume breach."

Rather than assuming that the perimeter defenses are impenetrable, organizations operate under the assumption that an attacker may already be inside the network.

This mindset shift leads to enhanced monitoring, continuous threat hunting, and a more proactive stance in identifying and mitigating threats.

Incident response teams are also adapting by becoming more cross-functional.

Collaboration between IT, security, legal, and compliance teams is essential in responding to modern threats effectively.

A multidisciplinary approach ensures that all aspects of an incident, including technical, legal, and regulatory, are addressed comprehensively.

Moreover, organizations are increasingly using tabletop exercises and simulations to test and refine their incident response plans.

These exercises allow teams to practice responding to various types of incidents, ensuring that everyone is familiar with their roles and responsibilities.

Communication is a critical element of modern incident response.

Clear and timely communication with internal and external stakeholders is essential for managing an incident's impact and reputation.

Organizations must establish communication protocols and define roles for communicating with employees, customers, partners, regulatory bodies, and the public.

Furthermore, modern incident response strategies recognize the importance of post-incident analysis and learning.

After an incident is resolved, it's crucial to conduct a thorough review to understand what happened, how it happened, and what can be done to prevent a recurrence.

This "lessons learned" approach helps organizations continuously improve their incident response capabilities.

In summary, adapting incident response strategies for modern threats is essential for organizations seeking to protect their digital assets and sensitive data.

Modern incident response encompasses proactive threat hunting, threat intelligence integration, machine learning and AI, containment measures, the "assume breach" mindset, cross-functional collaboration, tabletop exercises, effective communication, and post-incident analysis.

By embracing these elements, organizations can enhance their resilience and effectively respond to the evolving cybersecurity landscape.

BOOK 3
DIGITAL FORENSICS FOR BLUE TEAMS
ADVANCED TECHNIQUES AND INVESTIGATIONS

ROB BOTWRIGHT

Chapter 1: Foundations of Digital Forensics

The history and evolution of digital forensics trace the development of a field that has become indispensable in modern crime investigation and cybersecurity.

Digital forensics, also known as cyber forensics or computer forensics, emerged in response to the increasing use of computers and digital technologies in criminal activities.

The roots of digital forensics can be traced back to the late 1960s and early 1970s when law enforcement agencies recognized the potential value of computers as sources of evidence.

During this period, computer crime units were established to investigate cases involving mainframe computers and early personal computers.

One of the seminal moments in the field's history came in 1978 when the U.S. Secret Service established its first computer crime unit to investigate financial crimes involving computers.

Throughout the 1980s and 1990s, digital forensics continued to evolve as technology advanced.

The proliferation of personal computers and the advent of the internet created new opportunities for criminals and, consequently, new challenges for law enforcement.

In 1984, Fred Cohen, a pioneer in computer forensics, introduced the concept of computer viruses, which added a new layer of complexity to digital investigations.

By the late 1980s, the field began to distinguish between two primary branches: computer forensics and network forensics.

Computer forensics focused on analyzing data stored on computers and digital devices, while network forensics concentrated on investigating network traffic and communications.

The development of forensic software tools, such as EnCase and FTK (Forensic Toolkit), in the late 1990s greatly facilitated the extraction and analysis of digital evidence.

These tools provided investigators with the means to recover deleted files, examine hard drives, and analyze file metadata.

The early 2000s witnessed significant advancements in mobile device forensics as cell phones and smartphones became ubiquitous.

Digital forensics experts began developing techniques to extract data from mobile devices, including call records, text messages, and app data.

The proliferation of digital evidence in criminal cases led to the need for standardization and best practices in digital forensics.

In 2001, the National Institute of Standards and Technology (NIST) published the first edition of the "Guide to Computer Forensics and Investigations," which provided guidelines for conducting digital investigations.

The 21st century brought further evolution with the rise of cloud computing and the storage of data in remote servers.

Cloud forensics emerged as a specialized subfield focused on retrieving evidence from cloud-based services and storage platforms.

As the digital landscape continued to evolve, so did the methods used by criminals.

Cybercriminals became increasingly sophisticated, employing encryption, anti-forensics techniques, and anonymization tools to cover their tracks.

This prompted digital forensics professionals to enhance their skills and tools to keep pace with evolving threats.

In recent years, the importance of digital forensics has expanded beyond law enforcement.

Corporations and private organizations now employ digital forensics experts to investigate data breaches, insider threats, and other cybersecurity incidents.

Digital forensics has also become a vital component in civil litigation, where electronic evidence plays a crucial role in resolving disputes.

The field continues to evolve with the introduction of new technologies, such as blockchain and IoT (Internet of Things), each presenting unique challenges and opportunities for digital investigators.

Moreover, the growing importance of privacy and data protection regulations, such as GDPR, has added complexity to digital investigations, requiring professionals to navigate legal and ethical considerations.

In summary, the history and evolution of digital forensics reflect its transformation from a niche discipline to an essential component of modern criminal investigations, cybersecurity, and civil litigation.

From its early roots in computer crime units to its current role in addressing complex cyber threats and privacy concerns, digital forensics has continually adapted to meet the challenges of the digital age.

Legal and ethical considerations are paramount in the field of digital forensics, shaping the way investigators conduct their work and handle digital evidence.

In the digital age, the boundaries of privacy, data ownership, and individual rights have become increasingly complex and intertwined with forensic practices.

One of the foundational principles of digital forensics is the adherence to legal and ethical standards when acquiring, analyzing, and presenting digital evidence.

Digital forensics experts must operate within the boundaries set by national and international laws, as well as ethical guidelines established by professional organizations.

The legal landscape for digital forensics varies from country to country and even within different regions.

One common legal principle is the requirement for investigators to obtain proper authorization before conducting a digital investigation or seizing digital devices.

This authorization may come in the form of a search warrant, court order, or consent from the device's owner, depending on the circumstances.

Respecting the Fourth Amendment of the United States Constitution, for example, requires law enforcement to obtain a search warrant based on probable cause before conducting searches and seizures of digital devices.

In addition to authorization, the chain of custody is a critical legal consideration in digital forensics.

Maintaining a clear and documented chain of custody ensures that the integrity and admissibility of digital evidence are preserved throughout the investigative process.

Any break in the chain of custody could raise doubts about the evidence's reliability and admissibility in court.

Furthermore, digital forensics experts must ensure that their tools and methodologies comply with applicable laws and regulations.

For example, the use of forensic software and hardware should not violate software licensing agreements or intellectual property rights.

Ethical considerations in digital forensics extend beyond the legal framework and address issues related to professional conduct and responsibility.

One fundamental ethical principle is the duty to act impartially and without bias during the investigation.

Digital forensic professionals must avoid jumping to conclusions or making unfounded assumptions about the evidence they encounter.

Maintaining objectivity and neutrality is essential to preserving the integrity of the investigation.

Another ethical challenge in digital forensics is the preservation of privacy rights.

Investigators must strike a delicate balance between their duty to uncover evidence and the need to respect the privacy of individuals whose data is being examined.

This balance is particularly crucial in cases involving personal devices and sensitive information.

In addition to privacy concerns, digital forensics experts must consider the potential impact of their work on individuals' lives.

The consequences of a digital investigation can be far-reaching, affecting careers, reputations, and personal relationships.

Maintaining professionalism and discretion is essential to minimize harm to those involved.

Transparency and honesty are also ethical imperatives in digital forensics.

Investigators must accurately document their findings and report them truthfully, even if the evidence does not support a particular hypothesis or narrative.

Misrepresenting or concealing information can have severe ethical and legal consequences.

As technology continues to evolve, ethical considerations in digital forensics become more complex.

Emerging technologies, such as artificial intelligence and machine learning, raise questions about their use in automated data analysis and potential biases in algorithms.

Furthermore, the proliferation of digital evidence from social media, cloud storage, and IoT devices presents new challenges for preserving privacy and ensuring lawful access to information.

In summary, legal and ethical considerations are integral to the practice of digital forensics.

Adhering to legal standards, maintaining ethical conduct, preserving privacy, and upholding professional responsibility are essential elements of conducting digital investigations with integrity and fairness.

Navigating the ever-changing landscape of digital technologies while respecting legal and ethical boundaries is a fundamental aspect of the work carried out by digital forensics professionals.

Chapter 2: Evidence Acquisition and Preservation

Digital evidence collection methods are the techniques and procedures used to gather and preserve electronic evidence in a legally admissible and forensically sound manner.

In today's digital world, where information is often stored electronically, the ability to collect and analyze digital evidence is crucial for criminal investigations, civil litigation, and cybersecurity incidents.

One of the primary methods of digital evidence collection is acquiring data from electronic devices.

This process involves creating a forensic image or copy of the device's storage media, such as a hard drive or mobile phone, to ensure the original data remains unchanged.

Forensic imaging tools, like EnCase, FTK Imager, and dd (a command-line tool), are commonly used for this purpose.

The goal is to preserve the state of the device at the time of collection, allowing investigators to examine the data without altering or damaging it.

When collecting digital evidence from computers or mobile devices, it's essential to follow a well-defined protocol that includes documenting the device's make and model, its condition, and any potential security measures, such as passwords or encryption.

Network-based evidence collection is another crucial method, especially in cybersecurity incidents.

Network traffic, logs, and packets can provide valuable information about cyberattacks, data breaches, and network intrusions.

Network-based evidence collection tools, such as Wireshark and Snort, capture and analyze network data to identify suspicious or malicious activities.

Preserving the integrity of network evidence is critical, and investigators should ensure that timestamps and chain of custody information are accurately recorded.

Cloud-based evidence collection has become increasingly important as more data is stored in remote servers and cloud services.

To collect digital evidence from the cloud, investigators must use legal processes and follow cloud service providers' terms of service.

This may involve requesting data from cloud storage providers, such as Google Drive or Dropbox, through proper legal channels, including subpoenas or search warrants.

Social media platforms, too, can be a source of digital evidence.

In cases involving cyberbullying, harassment, or online threats, social media posts, messages, and user profiles may be collected as evidence.

While screenshots and manual data entry are often used to capture social media evidence, specialized tools can automate the process and ensure the authenticity of the data.

In cases involving digital evidence from IoT (Internet of Things) devices, such as smart home appliances or wearables, investigators must understand the unique challenges these devices present.

IoT devices may have limited storage and processing capabilities, making it crucial to collect data in a timely manner.

Moreover, data from IoT devices may be transmitted to the cloud or other servers, which requires different collection methods.

Forensic experts may need to work closely with manufacturers or developers to access and analyze data from IoT devices.

Digital evidence collection in the context of mobile forensics is a specialized area.

Mobile devices, including smartphones and tablets, contain a wealth of data, including call logs, text messages, photos, and app data.

Investigators use mobile forensic tools, like Cellebrite and Oxygen Forensic Detective, to extract and analyze data from mobile devices.

Proper chain of custody is essential when dealing with mobile devices, as they are often moved or powered down during investigations, potentially altering the evidence.

Additionally, geolocation data collected from mobile devices can be significant in criminal cases, providing information about a suspect's movements at specific times.

Vehicle forensics is yet another emerging area of digital evidence collection.

Modern vehicles are equipped with computer systems that record data about driving behavior, accidents, and GPS coordinates.

Digital evidence collected from vehicles can be valuable in accident reconstruction, criminal investigations, and insurance claims.

In summary, digital evidence collection methods encompass a wide range of techniques and procedures tailored to the diverse sources of digital data.

Whether collecting evidence from electronic devices, network traffic, cloud services, social media platforms, IoT devices, mobile devices, or vehicles, investigators must adhere to established protocols, maintain the integrity of the evidence, and follow legal and ethical guidelines.

Digital evidence collection is a critical aspect of modern forensic science and cybersecurity, allowing investigators to uncover the truth in an increasingly digital world.

Preserving digital evidence is a fundamental step in the investigative process, ensuring that the information collected remains accurate, authentic, and admissible in legal proceedings.

To achieve effective evidence preservation, investigators and forensic professionals must adhere to best practices and established protocols.

One of the primary best practices for evidence preservation is creating a clear and well-documented chain of custody.

A chain of custody is a chronological record that details the handling, storage, and transfer of evidence from the moment it's collected until it's presented in court.

This record includes information about who collected the evidence, when and where it was collected, and who had access to it at various stages of the investigation.

Maintaining an unbroken chain of custody is critical for establishing the authenticity and integrity of the evidence.

In addition to documenting the chain of custody, digital evidence should be stored in a secure and controlled environment.

This environment should protect the evidence from physical damage, unauthorized access, tampering, and environmental factors like temperature and humidity.

Evidence storage facilities should be equipped with security measures such as access controls, surveillance, and fire suppression systems.

Furthermore, digital evidence should be stored on non-alterable media, such as write-protected hard drives or write-once optical discs.

This prevents unintentional changes to the evidence during storage.

For digital devices like computers and mobile phones, investigators should follow strict procedures when acquiring and preserving evidence.

Forensic imaging, as previously discussed, is the process of creating an exact copy of the device's storage media.

This forensic image is the primary piece of evidence, and it should be stored separately from the original device.

Write-blocking hardware or software should be used during imaging to ensure that no data is altered during the process.

Moreover, investigators should document the hardware and software tools used during the acquisition process to demonstrate that the process was conducted properly and without alteration.

When handling digital evidence, it's essential to avoid actions that could compromise its integrity.

For example, investigators should refrain from booting up a suspect's computer or attempting to access password-protected files without proper authorization.

Such actions can potentially alter or destroy evidence and may not be admissible in court.

Instead, forensic experts should work with specialized tools and techniques designed for evidence preservation and analysis. Documentation is a key aspect of evidence preservation. Investigators should maintain detailed records of all actions taken during the investigation, from initial collection to analysis.

These records should include timestamps, descriptions of actions, and the names of individuals involved.

Maintaining clear and organized documentation ensures transparency and accountability in the investigative process.

When dealing with digital evidence stored in the cloud or on remote servers, investigators should follow legal processes and obtain proper authorization to access and collect the data.

Cloud service providers often have their own terms of service and procedures for responding to law enforcement requests, which investigators must adhere to.

Furthermore, investigators should make use of encryption and hashing techniques to protect digital evidence during transmission and storage.

Encrypting evidence during transmission ensures that it cannot be intercepted or altered by unauthorized parties.

Hashing, on the other hand, involves generating a unique cryptographic fingerprint (hash value) for digital files.

By comparing hash values before and after evidence collection, investigators can verify the integrity of the data.

Periodic validation of evidence is another best practice for preservation.

This involves rechecking the integrity of evidence at different stages of the investigation to ensure that it has not been tampered with or altered.

Validation can involve comparing hash values, verifying chain of custody records, and conducting forensic analysis to detect any signs of manipulation.

In summary, best practices for evidence preservation are essential for maintaining the integrity, authenticity, and admissibility of digital evidence in legal proceedings.

Creating a clear chain of custody, securing evidence storage, using proper acquisition procedures, avoiding actions that could compromise evidence, documenting all actions, following legal processes, and implementing encryption and hashing techniques are all vital components of effective evidence preservation.

By adhering to these best practices, investigators and forensic professionals can ensure that digital evidence remains credible and reliable throughout the investigative process.

Chapter 3: Memory Forensics and Volatile Data Analysis

Understanding memory forensics is crucial for digital investigators and cybersecurity professionals seeking to uncover critical information about a system's state, user activity, and potential security breaches.

Memory forensics, also known as volatile data analysis, involves examining a computer's RAM (Random Access Memory) to extract valuable information that may not be available through traditional disk-based forensics.

RAM is a temporary storage location for data that a computer's CPU (Central Processing Unit) actively uses during its operation.

Unlike data stored on a hard drive or SSD (Solid-State Drive), which persists even when the computer is powered off, RAM is volatile and loses its contents when the system is shut down or restarted.

This characteristic makes RAM a valuable source of information for investigators because it contains active processes, open network connections, running applications, and more, providing insights into the current state of a system.

Memory forensics allows investigators to analyze a wide range of volatile data, such as running processes, network connections, system configurations, and artifacts related to user activities, including passwords, encryption keys, and more.

One of the primary goals of memory forensics is to identify and analyze malicious or suspicious activities that may have occurred on a system.

Malware often resides in a system's memory to avoid detection by traditional antivirus software and to maintain persistence.

By examining RAM, investigators can discover the presence of malicious processes, rootkits, and other signs of compromise.

Memory analysis also plays a vital role in incident response, allowing organizations to quickly identify and respond to security incidents.

When a potential breach is detected, memory forensics can help investigators determine the extent of the compromise, identify the attacker's tactics, techniques, and procedures (TTPs), and collect valuable evidence for further analysis and legal action.

Memory forensics tools and techniques have evolved over the years, and today, there are several specialized tools designed to assist investigators in extracting and analyzing volatile data.

One popular tool in the field of memory forensics is Volatility.

Volatility is an open-source framework that provides a wide range of plugins for analyzing memory dumps from various operating systems, including Windows, Linux, and macOS.

Investigators can use Volatility to extract information such as process listings, open network connections, loaded kernel modules, and more.

Another notable tool is Rekall, which is also open source and highly extensible, offering a powerful platform for memory analysis.

Rekall allows investigators to create custom plugins and automate the analysis of memory dumps.

When performing memory forensics, investigators typically start by acquiring a memory dump from the target system.

This involves creating a snapshot of the system's RAM, which can be done using various methods, including live acquisition tools, such as LiME (Linux Memory Extractor), or by extracting the memory from a hibernation file (hiberfil.sys) on a Windows system.

Once a memory dump is obtained, investigators can then load it into a memory forensics tool, like Volatility or Rekall, and begin the analysis process.

Memory analysis can reveal a wealth of information about a system's activities.

For example, it can provide insights into the execution of malicious code, the identification of compromised user accounts, the presence of hidden processes, and even the extraction of encryption keys used to secure sensitive data.

In addition to identifying malicious activity, memory forensics can be used for other investigative purposes, such as recovering artifacts related to user interactions with the system.

These artifacts can include chat conversations, web browsing history, clipboard contents, and even decrypted data from encrypted communications.

Memory forensics can also assist in the reconstruction of events leading up to a system compromise or security incident.

By analyzing memory snapshots taken at different points in time, investigators can piece together a timeline of activities, helping them understand the sequence of events and identify potential attack vectors.

Memory analysis can be especially valuable in cases involving advanced threats and targeted attacks, where attackers often employ sophisticated techniques to avoid detection and persistence on a compromised system.

In such cases, memory forensics can uncover subtle indicators of compromise that may go unnoticed by traditional security measures.

However, it's important to note that memory forensics is a specialized skill that requires a deep understanding of operating system internals, memory structures, and the capabilities of memory analysis tools.

Investigators must be trained and experienced in this field to effectively use memory forensics techniques to uncover critical evidence and support incident response efforts.

In summary, understanding memory forensics is essential for digital investigators and cybersecurity professionals seeking to uncover valuable information hidden within a computer's RAM.

Memory analysis can reveal malicious activities, compromised user accounts, encryption keys, and artifacts related to user interactions, making it a vital tool for incident response and forensic investigations.

By employing specialized memory forensics tools and techniques, investigators can uncover critical evidence and gain insights into complex security incidents, ultimately enhancing their ability to detect, respond to, and mitigate cyber threats.

Analyzing volatile data in memory is a critical aspect of digital forensics and incident response, enabling investigators to uncover valuable insights into a system's current state and potential security incidents.

Volatile data, also known as live data, resides in a computer's RAM (Random Access Memory) and includes information about running processes, network connections, system configurations, and user activities.

Unlike data stored on disk drives, volatile data is temporary and is lost when the computer is powered off or restarted, making its timely analysis essential for incident response.

To analyze volatile data effectively, investigators employ various techniques and tools designed to extract and interpret this data.

One common technique is memory imaging, which involves capturing a snapshot of the system's RAM at a specific point in time.

Memory imaging can be done using specialized tools, such as LiME (Linux Memory Extractor) for Linux systems or WinPmem for Windows systems.

Once the memory image is acquired, investigators can load it into memory forensics tools like Volatility or Rekall to begin their analysis.

The first step in analyzing volatile data is often memory triage, where investigators quickly identify and prioritize critical artifacts for further examination.

Triage involves looking for signs of malicious activity, such as suspicious processes, network connections to known malicious IPs, or indicators of compromise (IOCs) provided by threat intelligence sources.

Investigators must also consider the context in which the system is used, as this can help identify normal versus abnormal behavior.

For example, a web server's memory should contain different artifacts compared to a standard user workstation.

Once critical artifacts are identified, investigators can delve deeper into memory analysis, using specialized plugins and techniques to extract valuable information.

Processes are a central focus of memory analysis, as they provide insights into what is actively running on the system.

Investigators can examine process listings, parent-child relationships, command-line arguments, and associated libraries to identify any malicious or suspicious activity.

Network connections found in volatile data can also be significant indicators of compromise.

Analyzing network connections can reveal communication with known malicious IPs, unusual ports, or traffic patterns indicative of a security incident.

In-memory artifacts related to user activity are another valuable aspect of memory analysis.

This includes items like clipboard contents, registry hives, and user profiles, which may contain sensitive information or clues about user actions.

For example, clipboard data can reveal text snippets copied by the user, which may include passwords or confidential information.

Similarly, examining user profiles can provide insights into recent user activity, such as recently accessed files or applications.

Memory analysis tools often provide specialized plugins for these tasks, making it easier for investigators to extract and interpret relevant information.

Kernel-level artifacts, such as loaded drivers and modules, are also crucial elements of memory analysis.

Malicious or unsigned drivers can indicate tampering with the operating system, while rootkit-like behavior may be evident in stealthy kernel-level code execution.

Investigators should scrutinize these artifacts to detect signs of compromise or unauthorized system manipulation.

Malware often employs evasion techniques to hide its presence in memory, making memory analysis even more challenging.

Rootkits, for instance, may use Direct Kernel Object Manipulation (DKOM) to tamper with the internal data structures of the kernel, making their presence difficult to detect.

To address this, memory forensics tools employ various techniques to detect and analyze these stealthy threats.

One such technique is memory integrity verification, which involves comparing the memory image's content with the expected behavior of the operating system.

Unexpected or anomalous behavior can indicate the presence of hidden processes or kernel-level modifications.

Timeline analysis is another powerful method in memory analysis. By reconstructing a timeline of activities using volatile data, investigators can understand the sequence of events leading up to a security incident. This can include identifying the initial infection vector, tracking lateral movement within the network, and determining what actions the attacker took on the compromised system.

Memory analysis is not limited to individual systems; it can also extend to memory dumps acquired from network appliances, routers, and other devices.

These memory dumps can contain information about network traffic, device configurations, and potential signs of compromise.

By analyzing volatile data from network devices, investigators can gain insights into network-based attacks and incidents.

In summary, analyzing volatile data in memory is a crucial skill for digital forensic professionals and incident responders.

Volatile data contains a wealth of information about a system's state and potential security incidents, making it a valuable source of evidence.

To analyze volatile data effectively, investigators use memory imaging, triage techniques, specialized tools, and a deep understanding of memory artifacts and evasion techniques employed by malware.

By uncovering and interpreting the information within volatile data, investigators can detect, respond to, and mitigate security incidents, ultimately enhancing the security posture of organizations and protecting against cyber threats.

Chapter 4: File System Analysis and Recovery

File system structures and analysis tools are essential components of digital forensics, enabling investigators to extract valuable evidence from storage media like hard drives, solid-state drives, and removable storage devices.

To understand how file system structures and analysis tools work, it's important to first grasp the fundamental concepts behind file systems and their organization.

A file system is a method used by operating systems to manage and store data on storage devices, such as disks.

It organizes data into files and directories, facilitating data retrieval and storage.

Common file systems include NTFS (New Technology File System) for Windows, ext4 for Linux, and HFS+ for macOS.

Each file system has its own way of organizing and managing data, resulting in unique structures that forensic investigators must navigate and analyze.

File system analysis tools play a crucial role in examining these structures, allowing investigators to uncover evidence relevant to digital investigations.

One essential concept in file systems is the partition, which is a logically separate section of a storage device.

Partitions help organize and manage data, and they can contain file systems.

For example, a computer's hard drive may have multiple partitions, each with its own file system.

To analyze a file system, investigators first need to access the storage device containing it.

This often involves creating a forensic image of the device, which is an exact copy of the original, preserving its data integrity.

Forensic imaging tools like dd (disk dump) and FTK Imager are commonly used for this purpose.

Once a forensic image is created, investigators can use file system analysis tools to examine its contents.

These tools help investigators navigate the file system's structures and recover files and metadata, such as file names, timestamps, and permissions.

One fundamental structure in file systems is the directory, which is a container for files and other directories.

Directories are organized in a hierarchical tree-like structure, with a root directory at the top.

File system analysis tools provide the ability to explore this directory structure, listing its contents and allowing investigators to access files and directories of interest.

File allocation is another critical aspect of file systems.

It determines how data is stored on the storage device.

File system analysis tools help investigators understand how files are allocated, which can be crucial when recovering deleted files or investigating file manipulation.

One common method of file allocation is through clusters or blocks.

Files are divided into clusters, and each cluster can hold a specific amount of data.

File system analysis tools assist in locating clusters associated with files, making it possible to reconstruct files even when they have been partially overwritten.

File metadata, such as timestamps, permissions, and file attributes, is valuable in digital investigations.

File system analysis tools extract and display this metadata, providing investigators with essential information about files and their history.

Metadata can reveal when a file was created, modified, or accessed, aiding in the establishment of a timeline of events.

File system journaling is a feature found in many modern file systems.

It records changes made to the file system in a journal or log, allowing for easy recovery in case of system crashes or failures.

File system analysis tools can access and interpret these journals, helping investigators understand what changes have occurred on the file system and when they occurred.

One commonly used file system analysis tool is The Sleuth Kit (TSK), which is an open-source software library and collection of command-line digital forensic tools.

TSK provides a range of utilities for file system analysis, including tools for listing directory structures, extracting file data, and recovering deleted files.

Another widely used tool is Autopsy, a graphical interface built on top of The Sleuth Kit.

Autopsy simplifies the process of file system analysis and allows investigators to visualize file system structures, view file metadata, and conduct keyword searches.

These tools are invaluable for forensic professionals and law enforcement agencies conducting digital investigations, as they help uncover evidence, build cases, and provide valuable insights into the activities of individuals and organizations.

In summary, file system structures and analysis tools are fundamental to the field of digital forensics.

Understanding how file systems organize and store data, as well as using the right analysis tools, empowers investigators to extract crucial evidence from storage devices and uncover the truth in digital investigations.

These tools play a vital role in law enforcement, cybersecurity, and incident response, contributing to the ongoing effort to combat cybercrime and protect digital assets.

Data recovery techniques for file systems are essential for restoring lost or deleted data from storage devices, providing a lifeline when critical information is at risk.

When data is inadvertently deleted or becomes inaccessible due to corruption or hardware failures, data recovery techniques can help salvage valuable information.

Next, we will explore various data recovery techniques used to recover files from file systems, including common tools and methods employed by professionals.

One commonly used data recovery technique involves the use of file recovery software, which is designed to scan storage devices for recoverable files.

These software tools are capable of identifying deleted or lost files and can often restore them to their original state.

Notable file recovery software includes Recuva, PhotoRec, and EaseUS Data Recovery Wizard.

These tools are user-friendly and can be used by individuals who are not necessarily experts in data recovery.

Another data recovery technique is the use of professional data recovery services.

In cases where file recovery software is unable to restore data, or when the storage device has suffered physical damage, professional data recovery services can be the best option.

These services employ specialized equipment and expertise to recover data from severely damaged or compromised storage devices.

While professional data recovery services can be more costly than using software, they offer the highest chances of successful recovery, especially for critical data.

A key principle in data recovery is to act promptly once data loss is detected.

Continuing to use the affected storage device can lead to overwriting the deleted or lost data, making it more challenging to recover.

Therefore, it's crucial to stop using the device as soon as data loss is suspected and to begin the recovery process promptly.

File systems play a crucial role in data recovery, as they determine how data is organized and stored on the storage device.

Understanding the file system used on the affected device is essential for successful data recovery.

File systems like NTFS, FAT32, HFS+, and ext4 have different structures, and data recovery techniques may vary based on the specific file system.

For example, file recovery software designed for NTFS file systems may not be as effective when used on devices with different file systems.

When using file recovery software, it's important to select the tool that is compatible with the file system of the storage device.

Data recovery techniques also involve searching for deleted or lost files by examining the file system's metadata.

File metadata includes information such as file names, timestamps (creation, modification, and access), file size, and file attributes.

By analyzing this metadata, data recovery tools can identify files that have been deleted or lost and restore them to their original locations or to a specified recovery destination.

One crucial aspect of data recovery techniques is the ability to preview recovered files before finalizing the recovery process.

Previewing recovered files allows users to verify that the desired data is intact and in a usable state.

This step is especially important when recovering a large number of files or when the storage device contains a mix of relevant and irrelevant data.

File recovery software often provides a preview feature, enabling users to view the content of recovered files before deciding which ones to restore.

Data recovery techniques may also involve the use of advanced methods like disk imaging and sector-by-sector scans.

Disk imaging creates a bit-by-bit copy of the entire storage device, preserving the original data structure and enabling a more comprehensive recovery.

Sector-by-sector scans examine every sector on the storage device, searching for recoverable data even in damaged or overwritten areas.

These advanced techniques can be employed when standard file recovery methods are insufficient.

It's essential to consider the potential risks associated with data recovery techniques.

For instance, using file recovery software may result in the accidental overwriting of deleted data, making it unrecoverable.

To mitigate this risk, it's advisable to recover data to a different storage device, such as an external hard drive, to avoid further damage to the original device.

Furthermore, professional data recovery services should be chosen carefully, as unscrupulous providers may compromise the confidentiality and integrity of recovered data.

In summary, data recovery techniques are invaluable for retrieving lost or deleted files from storage devices.

Whether using file recovery software, professional data recovery services, or advanced methods like disk imaging, these techniques can be a lifeline in situations where data loss threatens to disrupt business operations or personal data integrity.

Understanding the file system, acting promptly, and carefully considering the recovery method are key principles that can maximize the chances of successful data recovery.

Chapter 5: Network Forensics and Traffic Analysis

Network data collection and analysis tools are essential components of modern cybersecurity and network management, enabling organizations to monitor and safeguard their network infrastructure effectively.

These tools play a crucial role in gathering data about network traffic, performance, and security, providing valuable insights that help organizations maintain the integrity and availability of their networks.

In this chapter, we will explore various network data collection and analysis tools, their functionalities, and their significance in maintaining a secure and efficient network environment.

One of the fundamental categories of network data collection tools is network traffic analysis tools.

These tools capture and analyze network traffic to provide visibility into data flows, network utilization, and potential anomalies.

Popular network traffic analysis tools include Wireshark, tcpdump, and PRTG Network Monitor.

Wireshark, for instance, is an open-source packet analyzer that allows users to inspect network packets in real-time, helping them identify network issues and security threats.

Another important aspect of network data collection is monitoring network performance.

Network performance monitoring tools track various performance metrics such as latency, bandwidth usage, and packet loss.

These tools help organizations identify bottlenecks, optimize network resources, and ensure a seamless user experience.

PRTG Network Monitor, for example, offers comprehensive network performance monitoring capabilities, allowing organizations to proactively address network issues before they impact operations.

Security is a top priority for any network, and network security monitoring tools are vital in this regard.

These tools monitor network traffic for signs of suspicious or malicious activity, helping organizations detect and respond to security incidents promptly.

Intrusion Detection Systems (IDS) and Intrusion Prevention Systems (IPS) are examples of network security monitoring tools that can identify and mitigate threats.

Security Information and Event Management (SIEM) solutions, such as Splunk and IBM QRadar, provide centralized log management and real-time threat detection capabilities, making them valuable assets in network security.

While network data collection and analysis tools are essential, it's important to consider scalability and the ability to handle large volumes of network data.

As network traffic continues to grow, organizations need tools that can scale with their needs without compromising performance.

Scalability ensures that network administrators can monitor and analyze data effectively, even in large and complex network environments.

Cloud-based network monitoring solutions like SolarWinds Network Performance Monitor offer the scalability required to keep pace with evolving network demands.

Network data collection and analysis tools also play a crucial role in compliance and reporting.

Organizations often need to demonstrate compliance with regulatory requirements by maintaining detailed records of network activity.

These tools can generate reports that provide insights into network performance, security, and compliance, facilitating audits and regulatory assessments.

Comprehensive reporting capabilities are particularly important for organizations in industries like healthcare and finance, where regulatory compliance is highly regulated.

In addition to performance monitoring, security, and compliance, network data collection and analysis tools can aid in troubleshooting network issues.

When network problems occur, these tools help network administrators identify the root causes quickly and take corrective actions to minimize downtime.

Having the ability to pinpoint issues and assess their impact on network performance is essential for maintaining business continuity.

Network data collection tools can also be categorized based on the data they collect and analyze.

For instance, NetFlow and sFlow analyzers focus on flow data, which provides insights into network traffic patterns, source and destination information, and protocol usage.

Flow data is valuable for network capacity planning, identifying unauthorized network activities, and detecting Distributed Denial of Service (DDoS) attacks.

On the other hand, Deep Packet Inspection (DPI) tools analyze the content of network packets, allowing for detailed examination of data payloads.

DPI is commonly used for application performance monitoring, as it can reveal issues related to specific applications or services.

Network administrators can use DPI to ensure that mission-critical applications receive the necessary resources and that non-essential traffic does not negatively impact performance.

Network data collection and analysis tools also support the implementation of Quality of Service (QoS) policies.

These policies prioritize network traffic based on specific criteria, ensuring that critical applications receive the necessary bandwidth and latency requirements.

QoS is crucial in environments where voice and video communications must be given priority to maintain high-quality user experiences.

Tools like SolarWinds NetFlow Traffic Analyzer can help organizations implement and monitor QoS policies effectively.

In summary, network data collection and analysis tools are indispensable for organizations seeking to maintain secure, efficient, and compliant network environments.

These tools provide insights into network traffic, performance, and security, enabling proactive monitoring, troubleshooting, and optimization.

Whether it's monitoring network performance, enhancing security, or ensuring compliance, the right combination of network data collection and analysis tools is essential for the successful operation of modern networks.

Investigating network traffic patterns and anomalies is a crucial aspect of network management and cybersecurity.

Understanding how data flows within a network allows organizations to optimize performance and detect potential security threats.

Network traffic patterns refer to the typical data transfer and communication behaviors within a network.

These patterns can vary depending on the organization's size, industry, and specific network applications.

For instance, in a business environment, it's common to observe regular traffic patterns during working hours, with increased activity on weekdays and reduced activity on weekends.

However, patterns can also be influenced by external factors, such as holidays or events.

By analyzing these patterns, network administrators can identify baseline behavior and deviations from it.

Baseline behavior represents the expected network traffic under normal circumstances.

Deviations from this baseline can be indicative of network issues or security incidents.

One common tool for investigating network traffic patterns is NetFlow, which provides visibility into data flows within a network.

NetFlow records information about the source and destination of network traffic, the protocols used, and the amount of data transferred.

Analyzing NetFlow data can help organizations identify trends and patterns in network traffic.

For example, it can reveal which applications consume the most bandwidth, helping administrators make informed decisions about bandwidth allocation and Quality of Service (QoS) policies.

Moreover, NetFlow can assist in identifying suspicious activities, such as unexpected spikes in traffic or unusual communication patterns.

These anomalies may be signs of security threats or network performance issues.

In addition to NetFlow, organizations can utilize packet capture tools like Wireshark to investigate network traffic in more detail.

Packet capture tools capture individual network packets, allowing administrators to examine the content of data transmissions.

This level of visibility can be essential for diagnosing network issues and understanding the nature of traffic anomalies.

For instance, if a network is experiencing slow application performance, packet capture tools can help identify whether the issue is related to network latency, packet loss, or other factors.

Furthermore, packet capture can assist in detecting malicious activities, such as malware infections or network intrusions.

By analyzing packet contents, security analysts can identify patterns associated with known threats and take appropriate action.

Another aspect of investigating network traffic patterns is understanding the significance of peak traffic times.

Peak traffic occurs when network activity is at its highest, often during specific hours or events.

It's essential to monitor and analyze peak traffic times to ensure that network resources are allocated appropriately.

During peak times, bandwidth demand may exceed available capacity, leading to performance degradation.

Organizations can address this issue by implementing QoS policies that prioritize critical applications and allocate bandwidth accordingly.

Additionally, investigating peak traffic times can help organizations plan for network capacity upgrades if necessary.

It's important to note that investigating network traffic patterns is not solely about identifying deviations from normal behavior.

It's also about optimizing network performance and resource utilization.

By understanding how data flows within a network, organizations can make informed decisions about bandwidth allocation, hardware upgrades, and application optimization.

Moreover, monitoring network traffic patterns is an ongoing process.

Networks evolve over time, and so do the traffic patterns within them.

New applications and services may be introduced, and user behavior can change.

Therefore, regular monitoring and analysis of network traffic are essential to adapt to these changes effectively.

Intrusion Detection Systems (IDS) and Intrusion Prevention Systems (IPS) are valuable tools for investigating network traffic anomalies from a security perspective.

These systems continuously monitor network traffic and compare it against known attack signatures and behavioral patterns.

If an IDS or IPS detects suspicious or malicious activity, it can trigger alerts or take preventive actions to stop an attack in progress.

Network administrators can investigate these alerts to understand the nature of the anomaly and assess its impact.

Moreover, many IDS and IPS solutions offer reporting capabilities, allowing organizations to maintain records of security incidents and responses.

In summary, investigating network traffic patterns and anomalies is a multifaceted task that involves understanding baseline behavior, identifying deviations, optimizing network performance, and enhancing security.

It requires the use of various tools and techniques, such as NetFlow analysis, packet capture, QoS policies, and intrusion detection systems.

By continuously monitoring and analyzing network traffic, organizations can maintain a robust and secure network infrastructure that meets their operational needs.

Chapter 6: Malware Analysis for Blue Teams

Malware analysis is a critical discipline within the field of cybersecurity, aimed at understanding and combating malicious software.

In this chapter, we will delve into the fundamentals of malware analysis, exploring its importance and the various techniques employed to dissect and analyze malware.

Malware, short for malicious software, encompasses a broad category of software designed with malicious intent.

These malicious programs can include viruses, worms, Trojans, ransomware, spyware, adware, and more.

The primary goal of malware is to compromise the integrity, confidentiality, or availability of a computer system or its data.

Understanding malware is crucial because it poses a significant threat to individuals, organizations, and even nations.

Malware can lead to data breaches, financial losses, system disruptions, and even compromise national security.

Malware authors are often motivated by financial gain, political objectives, espionage, or simply the thrill of causing harm.

To effectively combat malware, cybersecurity professionals employ various strategies, one of which is malware analysis.

Malware analysis involves dissecting malicious software to understand its functionality, behavior, and impact on systems.

By gaining insights into how malware operates, security experts can develop countermeasures, detect infections, and prevent future attacks.

There are three primary approaches to malware analysis: static analysis, dynamic analysis, and hybrid analysis.

Static analysis involves examining the malware's code and structure without executing it.

This method includes examining file headers, inspecting strings and code patterns, and identifying potential vulnerabilities or exploits.

Dynamic analysis, on the other hand, involves running the malware in a controlled environment, such as a virtual machine or sandbox, to observe its behavior.

This approach provides insights into the malware's actions, including its network communication, file system modifications, and interactions with other processes.

Hybrid analysis combines elements of both static and dynamic analysis to gain a comprehensive understanding of the malware's capabilities.

One of the essential tools in malware analysis is the use of a controlled environment, commonly referred to as a "sandbox."

A sandbox is an isolated environment where malware can be executed safely for dynamic analysis.

It allows analysts to monitor the malware's actions without risking damage to a real system.

Sandbox environments can record system calls, network traffic, file modifications, and registry changes initiated by the malware.

These logs aid in uncovering the malware's intentions and potential payloads.

Static analysis often begins with examining the malware's binary code.

Analysts use disassemblers and decompilers to transform the machine code into a more human-readable format.

This process helps identify functions, libraries, and system calls used by the malware.

Additionally, static analysis can identify known malware signatures by comparing the binary against antivirus and threat intelligence databases.

Another critical aspect of static analysis is examining the malware's resources, such as embedded files, configuration files, and encrypted strings.

These resources may contain valuable information about the malware's behavior and communication methods.

Furthermore, static analysis can help identify code obfuscation and evasion techniques used by malware authors to evade detection.

Dynamic analysis, as previously mentioned, involves executing the malware in a controlled environment.

This method provides valuable insights into the malware's runtime behavior.

One of the primary tools used for dynamic analysis is the debugger, which allows analysts to interact with the running malware, pause execution, and inspect memory and registers.

By setting breakpoints and watching memory changes, analysts can trace the malware's execution flow and identify key functions or routines.

Network monitoring tools are also essential for dynamic analysis, as they capture the malware's network traffic, revealing communication with command and control servers or data exfiltration.

Additionally, dynamic analysis can help identify evasion techniques, as malware often behaves differently when executed in a sandbox compared to a real system.

Malware analysts also leverage memory analysis to uncover hidden artifacts within the running processes and memory.

This technique can reveal malicious code injected into legitimate processes, rootkit-like behavior, and stealthy malware persistence mechanisms.

Moreover, memory analysis can expose the malware's encryption keys, configuration data, and payloads, providing a deeper understanding of its capabilities.

Hybrid analysis combines elements of both static and dynamic analysis.

It typically starts with a static analysis to gather initial information about the malware, such as its file structure and potential indicators of compromise.

Once the static analysis is complete, the malware is executed in a controlled environment for dynamic analysis.

The hybrid approach provides a more comprehensive view of the malware's behavior and capabilities.

Throughout the malware analysis process, analysts document their findings, create reports, and share their knowledge with the cybersecurity community.

This collaborative effort helps develop detection signatures, update antivirus databases, and enhance security measures.

Malware analysis is a continually evolving field due to the ever-changing nature of malware.

Malware authors constantly adapt their techniques to evade detection, making it essential for analysts to stay updated on the latest malware trends and evasion tactics.

In summary, malware analysis is a critical component of cybersecurity that helps uncover the inner workings of malicious software.

Through static, dynamic, and hybrid analysis approaches, cybersecurity professionals gain insights into malware behavior, allowing for improved detection, prevention, and mitigation strategies.

This ongoing effort is essential to protect individuals and organizations from the pervasive threat posed by malware in today's digital landscape.

Dynamic and static analysis are two fundamental techniques used in cybersecurity and software engineering to examine and understand the behavior and structure of computer programs, applications, and software systems. Dynamic analysis, as the name suggests, involves the observation and assessment of a program's behavior while it's running or executing in a real or controlled environment. This technique is primarily concerned with runtime characteristics and interactions.

In contrast, static analysis focuses on the examination of a program's code, structure, and design without actually executing it. It's like studying a blueprint of a building to understand its architecture and design principles without going inside the building itself. Both dynamic and static analysis have their unique strengths and applications, and cybersecurity professionals often use them in combination to gain a comprehensive understanding of software and its potential security issues.

Let's delve deeper into these two analysis techniques, starting with dynamic analysis. In dynamic analysis, cybersecurity experts execute a program or software component in a controlled environment, often referred to as a sandbox or testing environment. This controlled environment allows for the observation of the program's behavior while minimizing potential risks to the host system.

One of the primary tools used in dynamic analysis is a debugger, which enables analysts to interact with the running program, pause its execution, inspect memory, and monitor the program's variables and registers. Debuggers are valuable for tracking the program's execution flow, identifying key functions, and pinpointing areas of interest within the program's code.

During dynamic analysis, analysts also employ network monitoring tools to capture and analyze network traffic generated by the program. This helps in understanding how the program communicates with external entities, such as servers or other networked devices. Analyzing network traffic can reveal potential security risks, such as unauthorized data transfers or suspicious connections to known malicious domains.

Another aspect of dynamic analysis involves observing the program's interactions with the host system's file system and registry. This helps identify any attempts by the program to modify files, create or delete registry keys, or engage in other potentially malicious activities. By closely monitoring these interactions, analysts can detect and analyze potentially harmful behaviors.

Furthermore, dynamic analysis can uncover the program's use of system resources, such as CPU and memory. This information can be critical in identifying resource-intensive or inefficient code that may lead to performance problems or security vulnerabilities.

Now, let's shift our focus to static analysis. In static analysis, cybersecurity experts examine a program's code and structure without executing it. The goal is to identify potential security issues, vulnerabilities, and design flaws by analyzing the program's source code, binary code, or intermediate representations. Static analysis tools play a significant role in this process.

One of the essential static analysis tools is the static code analyzer, which scans the program's source code or binary for known patterns, coding errors, and potential security vulnerabilities. These tools use predefined rulesets and algorithms to flag code segments that may require further inspection. Static code analyzers can identify issues such as buffer overflows, injection vulnerabilities, and unvalidated input handling.

Additionally, static analysis tools can provide insights into code complexity and maintainability, which are important factors in software security. Code that is overly complex or difficult to maintain may hide potential vulnerabilities or make it challenging to implement security updates effectively.

Static analysis can also include the examination of software dependencies and libraries. By analyzing the dependencies, cybersecurity professionals can identify potential security risks associated with third-party components or outdated libraries. These vulnerabilities can expose a program to attacks, such as those targeting known weaknesses in third-party software.

Another critical aspect of static analysis is the assessment of code quality and adherence to coding standards and best practices. Well-documented, well-structured code is more likely to be secure, as it is easier to review for vulnerabilities and maintain over time.

Furthermore, static analysis can help uncover potential design flaws, architectural issues, and code smells that may not be apparent during dynamic analysis. These issues can include poor data handling, insecure configurations, or improper error handling. Identifying such problems early in the development process can significantly improve software security.

In practice, cybersecurity professionals often combine both dynamic and static analysis techniques to perform comprehensive security assessments of software systems. This hybrid approach allows them to leverage the strengths of each technique while compensating for their respective limitations. By conducting thorough dynamic and static analyses, cybersecurity experts can uncover vulnerabilities, assess software security, and ultimately enhance the overall resilience of computer programs and systems.

In summary, dynamic and static analysis are essential techniques in the field of cybersecurity and software development. Dynamic analysis focuses on observing a program's behavior during execution, while static analysis involves scrutinizing the code and structure without execution. These techniques, used individually or in combination, enable cybersecurity professionals to identify security vulnerabilities, assess software quality, and enhance the security posture of software systems.

Chapter 7: Advanced Data Recovery Techniques

Data recovery from damaged storage media is a crucial and often challenging task in the realm of information technology. When storage devices like hard drives, solid-state drives, USB flash drives, or memory cards become damaged, the data they contain may be at risk of being lost permanently. Understanding the principles and techniques of data recovery from damaged storage media is essential for IT professionals and individuals alike.

One of the first steps in data recovery from damaged storage media is to assess the extent of the damage. Physical damage, such as a scratched or physically broken storage device, may require specialized equipment and cleanroom facilities to recover data effectively. On the other hand, logical damage, which refers to data corruption or file system issues, may be addressed through software-based recovery methods.

For physically damaged storage media, it is crucial to handle the device with care to prevent further harm. The use of proper anti-static precautions and protective gear can minimize the risk of electrostatic discharge (ESD) and contamination in the case of mechanical failures. Dust and debris within the storage device can exacerbate the damage, so cleanroom environments with controlled air quality are often employed for safe recovery operations.

Data recovery professionals may use specialized tools and equipment, such as head stack replacement tools and platter extraction tools, to address physical damage in hard drives. These tools allow technicians to access the data stored on the drive's platters, even when the drive's internal components are damaged.

In cases of logical damage, where the file system or data structure is compromised, software-based recovery methods are often employed. Data recovery software can scan the damaged storage media, identify recoverable files and directories, and then reconstruct the data. It's important to note that the success of software-based recovery largely depends on the extent of the damage and the effectiveness of the recovery software used.

When recovering data from damaged storage media, it's crucial to avoid writing any new data to the affected device. Writing new data can overwrite the space where the lost data was stored, making it irretrievable. Data recovery professionals often create a disk image or clone of the damaged media to work on, preserving the original state of the device for further recovery attempts.

File carving is another technique commonly used in data recovery, particularly for devices with corrupted or missing file system structures. File carving involves scanning the storage media for file signatures and extracting data fragments based on these signatures. While it can be effective in recovering individual files, it may not always be able to reconstruct the original directory structure or filenames.

In some cases, data recovery may require manual intervention. Skilled technicians can manually extract data from damaged storage media by carefully disassembling and accessing the storage components directly. This approach is often necessary when other recovery methods prove insufficient, but it should only be attempted by professionals with the appropriate expertise.

Data recovery specialists may also resort to firmware repair in cases where the storage device's firmware, which controls its operations, becomes corrupted. Firmware repair involves reprogramming or repairing the firmware to restore the device's functionality and recover the data.

It's important to note that not all data recovery attempts are successful. The outcome depends on factors such as the type and extent of damage, the quality of the recovery equipment and software used, and the expertise of the individuals performing the recovery. Therefore, it's advisable to seek professional assistance for critical data recovery tasks, as DIY attempts can potentially worsen the situation.

Regular backups play a crucial role in mitigating the impact of data loss due to damaged storage media. By maintaining up-to-date backups of important data, individuals and organizations can significantly reduce the risk of data loss and minimize the need for complex data recovery operations.

In summary, data recovery from damaged storage media is a complex and specialized field within information technology. Whether the damage is physical or logical, addressing it requires careful assessment, the use of appropriate tools and techniques, and often professional expertise. Data recovery professionals are trained to handle a wide range of storage media issues, but prevention through regular backups remains the most effective strategy for safeguarding valuable data.

Data carving and fragmented file recovery are essential techniques in the field of data forensics and data recovery. These methods play a crucial role in retrieving valuable information from storage media, particularly when files are fragmented or have been deleted.

In many instances, when a file is deleted from a storage device, it may not be completely eradicated. Instead, the file's data clusters may be marked as available for reuse, but the actual data remains intact until overwritten by new information. Data carving takes advantage of this fact by scanning the storage media for specific file signatures or headers, even when file system metadata is no longer available.

The process of data carving begins with identifying unique signatures or markers associated with specific file types. For example, a JPEG image file may have a distinctive header or magic number that indicates the start of the file. Similarly, a PDF document has a recognizable structure that can be used for identification.

Once these signatures are known, data carving software scans the storage media sector by sector, searching for instances where the signature matches the data at that location. When a match is found, the software begins carving out the data, including all the fragments that follow, until a defined endpoint or marker is reached.

Data carving is particularly effective in recovering fragmented files. Fragmentation occurs when a file's data is not stored in a contiguous block on the storage device. Instead, the file is broken into smaller pieces or fragments scattered throughout the media. This fragmentation can result from various factors, including the file system's allocation strategy and the frequent creation and deletion of files.

When a file is fragmented, its data may be spread across multiple sectors or clusters on the storage device. Traditional file recovery methods that rely on file system metadata may struggle to reconstruct such files accurately. Data carving, on the other hand, can identify and assemble these fragmented pieces, ultimately recovering the entire file.

One key advantage of data carving is its ability to recover files regardless of their file system. While file systems like NTFS, FAT, and HFS+ have their own data structures and metadata that facilitate file organization and retrieval, data carving operates at a lower level, making it file system agnostic. This means that it can be used to recover files from a wide range of storage media, regardless of the file system in use.

However, data carving is not without its challenges and limitations. It may yield false positives, where the software identifies data as belonging to a specific file type, but it turns out to be unrelated. This can result in the recovery of corrupted or incomplete files. Additionally, data carving may not always retrieve filenames or directory structures, making it challenging to organize and identify recovered files.

In cases where a storage device has been significantly damaged or overwritten with new data, data carving's success rate may diminish. When data clusters are reused or overwritten, the original file's fragments can be partially or entirely lost, reducing the chances of successful recovery.

To enhance the effectiveness of data carving, it's essential to use specialized software tools that are tailored to specific file types. For example, software designed for photo recovery may excel at recovering JPEG and RAW image files, while video recovery software may focus on AVI, MP4, or MOV files. These tools are often equipped with advanced algorithms that improve the accuracy of data carving and reduce false positives.

It's worth noting that data carving can be a time-consuming process, particularly on large storage devices or media with significant fragmentation. Patience and the use of efficient carving software are key to achieving successful results.

In summary, data carving is a valuable technique in the field of data forensics and recovery. It allows for the retrieval of files, even when their file system metadata is no longer available or when they are fragmented across the storage media. By identifying unique file signatures and assembling fragmented pieces, data carving software can recover a wide range of file types, making it an indispensable tool for data recovery specialists and forensic investigators. However, it's essential to be aware of its limitations and potential challenges, particularly in cases of extensive data damage or overwriting.

Chapter 8: Mobile Device Forensics

Mobile device forensics is a specialized field within digital forensics that focuses on the acquisition, analysis, and preservation of digital evidence from smartphones, tablets, and other mobile devices. As these devices have become an integral part of our daily lives, they have also become valuable sources of information in criminal investigations, civil litigation, and cybersecurity incidents.

The significance of mobile device forensics lies in the vast amount of data that can be stored on these devices. Smartphones, in particular, are like mini-computers that contain a treasure trove of information, including text messages, call logs, emails, photos, videos, location data, and app usage history. This data can provide critical insights into a person's activities, communications, and connections.

One of the fundamental principles of mobile device forensics is ensuring the integrity of the evidence. When handling a mobile device, it's crucial to follow proper procedures to preserve the data in a forensically sound manner. This includes using specialized tools and techniques to create a bit-for-bit copy of the device's storage, known as a forensic image. By creating a forensic image, investigators can work with the copy of the data, ensuring that the original evidence remains intact and unaltered.

The process of mobile device acquisition involves connecting the device to a computer using a forensic tool or cable. Once connected, the investigator can initiate the data extraction process, which may include accessing the device's file system, logical data, and physical data. Logical data includes the data that is accessible to the device's operating system and apps, while physical data includes all the data stored on the device's storage media.

Mobile device forensics also requires investigators to be knowledgeable about various operating systems, as different devices run on different platforms, such as iOS, Android, and Windows Mobile. Each platform has its own file systems, data storage mechanisms, and security features that must be understood and navigated during the forensic examination.

One of the challenges in mobile device forensics is dealing with encryption and security measures. Many modern smartphones are equipped with encryption to protect user data. Decrypting this data can be a complex and time-consuming process, and in some cases, it may not be possible to access certain encrypted data without the user's passcode or biometric authentication.

Another critical aspect of mobile device forensics is chain of custody. Maintaining a meticulous record of who has had access to the device and when is essential to ensure the admissibility of evidence in court. This chain of custody documentation helps establish that the evidence has not been tampered with or altered during the investigation.

Mobile device forensics extends beyond data acquisition. Once the data is extracted, it needs to be analyzed. This analysis involves examining the data for relevant information, connections, and patterns that may be of interest to an investigation. Investigators use specialized software tools to parse and interpret the data, helping them uncover evidence that can support a case.

In addition to data stored on the device itself, mobile device forensics also encompasses cloud-based data. Many mobile apps sync data to cloud services, such as iCloud or Google Drive. Investigating these cloud-based accounts can provide valuable insights into a user's activities and communications. This requires knowledge of cloud forensics techniques and the legal considerations surrounding cloud data.

Mobile device forensics is not limited to law enforcement and criminal investigations. It also plays a vital role in corporate investigations, internal audits, and eDiscovery processes. Organizations may need to examine mobile devices to uncover evidence of misconduct, intellectual property theft, or violations of company policies. In such cases, mobile device forensics can help establish a factual basis for taking appropriate actions.

In summary, mobile device forensics is a multifaceted field that involves the acquisition, analysis, and preservation of digital evidence from smartphones and other mobile devices. It requires a deep understanding of different operating systems, encryption methods, and chain of custody procedures. The insights gained from mobile device forensics can be invaluable in criminal investigations, civil litigation, corporate investigations, and cybersecurity incidents, making it a vital discipline in the broader field of digital forensics.

iOS and Android forensics are specialized areas within the field of mobile device forensics, focusing on the examination of Apple's iOS and Google's Android operating systems, which power the majority of smartphones and tablets in use today.

When conducting iOS and Android forensics, investigators are tasked with extracting and analyzing digital evidence from devices running these operating systems. The goal is to retrieve information that can be used in criminal investigations, legal proceedings, or cybersecurity incidents. This evidence may include text messages, call logs, emails, photos, videos, location data, and app-related information.

One of the first steps in iOS and Android forensics is obtaining physical access to the device. This can be achieved through various means, including consent from the device owner, a search warrant, or the use of specialized forensic tools. Once physical access is obtained, the forensic examiner creates a forensic image of the device's storage to ensure data integrity.

The forensic image is an exact copy of the device's storage, capturing both allocated and unallocated data sectors. This is essential because deleted or hidden data may still be recoverable from unallocated sectors, providing valuable clues in an investigation.

In iOS forensics, one of the key challenges is dealing with Apple's security mechanisms. iPhones and iPads are designed with robust security features, including hardware-based encryption. To access the data on an iOS device, forensic experts often need the device's passcode or biometric authentication, such as a fingerprint or facial recognition.

Additionally, Apple's ecosystem relies heavily on cloud services like iCloud, where user data is stored and synchronized. Forensic examiners must be knowledgeable about iCloud forensics and how to obtain data from the cloud, which can complement the data extracted directly from the device.

In Android forensics, the landscape is more diverse due to the wide range of device manufacturers and Android versions in use. Different manufacturers may implement various security features, making some devices more challenging to examine than others. Understanding these variations is crucial for a successful forensic analysis.

Both iOS and Android devices maintain detailed logs of user activities, such as call records, text messages, and app usage. Forensic examiners can leverage these logs to reconstruct timelines and uncover valuable evidence related to a case. Timestamps are essential for establishing the sequence of events.

App data analysis is another critical aspect of iOS and Android forensics. Mobile apps store a wealth of information, from chat messages to geolocation data. Forensic tools and techniques are used to extract, parse, and analyze this data, shedding light on a user's interactions and behaviors.

Location data, in particular, can be highly significant in investigations. Both iOS and Android devices track the user's location through GPS, cell tower data, and Wi-Fi network connections. This information can be used to establish a person's movements and whereabouts at specific times.

Digital evidence from mobile devices is often presented in court to support legal cases. Therefore, it's essential for forensic examiners to follow strict protocols and document their findings meticulously. Maintaining a chain of custody and ensuring that evidence remains unaltered is of paramount importance to ensure its admissibility in court.

In some cases, forensic experts may encounter challenges when dealing with locked or encrypted devices. Decryption may require specialized tools and techniques or cooperation from the device owner. Legal considerations and privacy concerns also play a role in these situations.

It's worth noting that iOS and Android forensics extend beyond smartphones and tablets. Wearable devices, such as smartwatches and fitness trackers, often sync data with mobile devices. Examining these wearables can provide additional insights into a user's activities and health data.

Furthermore, the ever-evolving nature of mobile technology means that forensic examiners must stay up to date with the latest advancements and security measures. New versions of iOS and Android may introduce changes in data storage, encryption, or security, necessitating adjustments in forensic techniques.

In summary, iOS and Android forensics are specialized disciplines within mobile device forensics, focusing on the examination of Apple and Google's mobile operating systems. Forensic examiners face challenges related to security features, encryption, cloud services, and diverse Android device models. Extracting and analyzing digital evidence from these devices is essential in criminal investigations, legal proceedings, and cybersecurity incidents, making iOS and Android forensics crucial components of modern forensic science.

Chapter 9: Cloud and Virtual Environment Forensics

Cloud forensics is a rapidly evolving field that addresses the challenges of investigating digital incidents that involve cloud computing environments.

With the widespread adoption of cloud services, individuals and organizations are increasingly storing data and running applications in remote data centers managed by cloud providers.

These cloud environments offer numerous benefits, such as scalability, accessibility, and cost-effectiveness.

However, they also introduce unique challenges for digital forensics investigators.

One of the primary challenges in cloud forensics is the decentralization of data.

Unlike traditional computing environments where data is stored on local devices or servers, in the cloud, data is distributed across multiple servers and data centers.

This means that when an incident occurs, investigators may need to access and analyze data that resides in various geographical locations.

Furthermore, cloud service providers often replicate data for redundancy and load balancing, making it even more complex to trace and recover digital evidence.

In addition to the geographical distribution of data, cloud forensics also faces issues related to the multi-tenancy of cloud environments.

In a multi-tenant cloud, multiple users or organizations share the same physical infrastructure and resources.

This shared environment raises concerns about data isolation, access control, and the potential for cross-contamination of evidence.

Digital forensics investigators must take these factors into account when collecting and analyzing data from a multi-tenant cloud.

Another challenge in cloud forensics is the dynamic nature of cloud computing.

Cloud resources can be provisioned and de-provisioned rapidly, and data can be moved or deleted without warning.

This dynamic environment can lead to the loss of critical evidence if investigators do not act quickly.

To address this challenge, forensic experts must employ real-time monitoring and data preservation techniques to ensure that evidence is captured before it is altered or deleted.

Cloud service providers also play a significant role in cloud forensics.

They control access to the cloud infrastructure and may have their own policies and procedures for responding to legal requests or incidents.

Investigators must work closely with cloud providers to obtain the necessary permissions and access to conduct their forensic investigations.

Furthermore, investigators should be aware that cloud providers may have limited retention periods for certain types of data, which can impact the availability of historical evidence.

In cloud forensics, data encryption is both a challenge and an opportunity.

Many cloud providers use encryption to protect data in transit and at rest.

While this encryption enhances security, it can complicate forensic investigations, as encrypted data may be unreadable without the encryption keys.

Digital forensics experts must employ techniques to recover encryption keys or analyze encrypted data, which requires specialized knowledge and tools.

Additionally, investigators should be aware of the legal and ethical considerations surrounding encryption and data privacy when conducting cloud forensics.

To overcome the challenges of cloud forensics, investigators employ various methods and techniques.

One key method is the use of forensic images.

Similar to traditional digital forensics, investigators create forensic images of cloud-based virtual machines, storage volumes, or containers.

These images capture the state of the cloud resources at a specific point in time and can be analyzed in a controlled environment.

Forensic images are essential for preserving evidence and ensuring that it remains unchanged during analysis.

Moreover, investigators use network packet analysis to examine network traffic between cloud resources and external entities.

This analysis can reveal communication patterns, data transfers, and potential security breaches.

Furthermore, investigators use log analysis to review logs generated by cloud services and applications.

Logs can provide valuable information about user activities, system events, and security incidents.

Advanced log analysis techniques, such as correlation and anomaly detection, help identify suspicious activities or security breaches.

Cloud forensics also benefits from the use of digital forensics tools and software.

These tools assist investigators in collecting, analyzing, and preserving evidence from cloud environments.

Some tools are specifically designed for cloud forensics, offering features tailored to the challenges of cloud computing.

Additionally, cloud providers offer management and monitoring tools that can assist investigators in tracking and analyzing cloud resources.

As cloud computing continues to evolve, so too will cloud forensics.

New challenges will arise as technology advances, and investigators must adapt to these changes.

Researchers and practitioners in the field of digital forensics are continually developing innovative methods and solutions to address emerging challenges in cloud forensics.

Ultimately, cloud forensics is essential for ensuring the integrity of digital evidence, investigating cybercrimes, and holding individuals and organizations accountable for their actions in the cloud.

Forensic analysis in virtualized environments has become increasingly important in the field of digital forensics.

Virtualization technology allows multiple virtual machines (VMs) to run on a single physical host, providing flexibility and resource optimization.

However, it also presents unique challenges for forensic investigators.

One of the primary challenges in virtualized environments is the dynamic nature of VMs.

VMs can be created, deleted, and migrated between hosts, making it challenging to track their movements and changes.

This dynamic behavior can complicate the process of collecting and preserving digital evidence.

Additionally, VMs often share the same physical hardware resources, such as CPU, memory, and storage.

As a result, it's possible for one VM to access and potentially compromise the data of another VM on the same host.

Digital forensics experts must consider the shared resource model of virtualization when conducting investigations.

Another challenge in virtualized environments is the need to analyze both the VM and the underlying physical host.

Investigators must examine the VM's file system, memory, and network traffic to gather evidence related to a specific incident.

Simultaneously, they need to analyze the host's logs, configurations, and hypervisor-level activities.

This dual analysis approach is crucial for understanding the full scope of an incident and determining its impact.

To address these challenges, forensic experts have developed specialized tools and techniques for virtualized environments.

One key technique is the use of snapshot technology.

Snapshots capture the state of a VM at a specific point in time, including its memory, disk, and configuration.

Forensic investigators can create snapshots before conducting any analysis to preserve the VM's state for examination.

This ensures that the VM remains unchanged during the investigation.

Moreover, investigators can use snapshot differencing to identify changes made to a VM after a snapshot was taken.

Another important aspect of forensic analysis in virtualized environments is memory analysis.

Memory analysis allows investigators to examine the contents of a VM's memory, which can contain valuable evidence.

Investigators can extract information such as running processes, open network connections, and encryption keys from memory.

Memory analysis tools are specifically designed to work in virtualized environments and can help uncover hidden or volatile evidence.

Furthermore, network analysis plays a significant role in virtualized forensic investigations.

Investigators can capture and analyze network traffic between VMs and external entities to identify communication patterns and potential security breaches.

Analyzing network traffic helps reconstruct the timeline of events and understand how an incident unfolded.

In virtualized environments, hypervisor-level forensics is crucial.

Hypervisors are responsible for managing VMs and their resources.

Forensic experts must examine hypervisor logs and configurations to understand VM movements, resource allocations, and potential security vulnerabilities at the host level.

Moreover, investigators need to verify the integrity of VM images.

Digital evidence collected from VMs should be validated to ensure its authenticity and reliability.

Hashing techniques can be used to verify the integrity of VM images, ensuring that they have not been tampered with.

In addition to technical challenges, legal and ethical considerations are essential in virtualized forensic analysis.

Investigators must obtain proper permissions and adhere to legal procedures when conducting forensic examinations in virtualized environments.

Moreover, the sharing of physical resources in virtualization raises concerns about data isolation and privacy.

Investigators should take measures to prevent cross-contamination of evidence and protect sensitive information.

As virtualization technology continues to evolve, so will the methods and tools used in virtualized forensic analysis.

Researchers and practitioners in the field of digital forensics are continually developing new techniques to address emerging challenges in virtualized environments.

Ultimately, forensic analysis in virtualized environments is essential for uncovering digital evidence, investigating cybercrimes, and ensuring the integrity of legal proceedings.

It requires a combination of technical expertise, specialized tools, and a thorough understanding of the complexities of virtualization technology.

Chapter 10: Cyber Attribution and Threat Intelligence

In the world of cybersecurity, attribution, or the process of identifying the individuals or entities behind cyberattacks, is a complex and challenging endeavor.

It's akin to trying to uncover the identity of a burglar who wears a mask, operates from a remote location, and leaves behind digital footprints that can be easily obfuscated.

Attribution is essential because it enables cybersecurity professionals and law enforcement agencies to respond effectively to cyber threats and hold cybercriminals accountable for their actions.

However, several factors contribute to the significant challenges in attributing cyberattacks.

Firstly, the anonymity provided by the internet allows malicious actors to hide their true identities.

Cybercriminals can use techniques like Tor, VPNs, and proxy servers to conceal their IP addresses and location, making it difficult to trace their origin.

Furthermore, attribution becomes even more complex when nation-state actors are involved.

State-sponsored cyberattacks often involve sophisticated techniques and extensive resources, making it challenging to attribute the attacks to a specific government agency or organization.

These actors are adept at using deception and misdirection to muddy the waters and throw investigators off their trail.

Additionally, cybercriminals can employ various tactics to obfuscate their tracks.

They may use compromised or infected machines as proxies, routing their attacks through multiple intermediaries to hide their true source.

They can also employ false flags, planting misleading clues to divert attention away from their actual identity.

Another challenge in attribution is the global nature of cyberattacks.

Cybercriminals can launch attacks from anywhere in the world, crossing international borders with ease.

This jurisdictional complexity makes it challenging for law enforcement agencies to coordinate investigations and apprehend suspects.

Furthermore, the attribution process often relies on technical indicators and digital forensic evidence.

However, these indicators can be manipulated or forged, making it necessary to corroborate technical evidence with other forms of intelligence.

Advanced persistent threats (APTs), for instance, are known for their ability to operate covertly over extended periods, evading detection and attribution.

These adversaries are skilled at remaining hidden within compromised networks, making it difficult for defenders to identify them.

Moreover, attribution challenges are exacerbated by the use of false personas and stolen credentials.

Cybercriminals can impersonate legitimate users or organizations, making it challenging to distinguish between authorized and malicious activity.

They can also leverage compromised accounts and infrastructure to launch attacks, making it appear as though the attacks originate from legitimate sources.

Additionally, the use of malware, such as remote access Trojans (RATs), enables cybercriminals to maintain persistent access to compromised systems while concealing their true identities.

Attribution is further complicated by the practice of threat actors collaborating with one another.

Cybercriminals may work in groups or share tactics, techniques, and procedures (TTPs) to confuse investigators and make it appear as though multiple actors are involved.

Furthermore, the use of ransomware and cryptocurrency for extortion has added a layer of complexity to attribution.

Ransomware attacks often demand cryptocurrency payments, which can be challenging to trace to a specific individual or entity.

Despite these challenges, efforts to improve attribution in cybersecurity continue to evolve.

Cybersecurity professionals are continually developing new techniques and tools to enhance the accuracy of attribution.

Collaboration among private sector organizations, law enforcement agencies, and international partners has become essential in tracking and identifying cybercriminals.

The sharing of threat intelligence and the establishment of cybersecurity information-sharing platforms have been instrumental in this regard.

Moreover, advancements in machine learning and artificial intelligence are aiding in the attribution process by analyzing vast amounts of data and identifying patterns and anomalies that may lead to the identification of threat actors.

Legal frameworks and international agreements are also being established to facilitate the extradition and prosecution of cybercriminals across borders.

In summary, attribution challenges in cybersecurity are significant but not insurmountable.

As cyber threats continue to evolve, the field of attribution will likewise advance, enabling organizations and law enforcement agencies to better identify and hold cybercriminals accountable for their actions.

While attribution may never be entirely straightforward, ongoing efforts and technological advancements are gradually improving our ability to uncover the identities behind cyberattacks.

In the ever-evolving landscape of cybersecurity, one of the most valuable assets for organizations and security professionals is threat intelligence.

Think of threat intelligence as a form of collective knowledge gathered from various sources to provide insights into the tactics, techniques, procedures, and motivations of cyber threat actors.

This intelligence helps organizations proactively defend against cyber threats and, in some cases, attribute attacks to specific actors or groups.

The value of threat intelligence lies in its ability to inform security teams about emerging threats and vulnerabilities that may affect their systems and networks.

By understanding the tactics and tools employed by cybercriminals, organizations can better prepare their defenses and respond more effectively to potential threats.

So, how does threat intelligence work, and how can it be leveraged for defense and attribution in the realm of cybersecurity?

To begin with, threat intelligence is not a one-size-fits-all concept.

There are different types of threat intelligence, each serving a unique purpose:

Strategic Threat Intelligence: This provides high-level insights into the long-term strategies and goals of threat actors. It helps organizations understand the broader threat landscape and make informed decisions about their security posture.

Operational Threat Intelligence: This focuses on the tactics, techniques, and procedures (TTPs) used by threat actors in specific campaigns. It helps security teams detect and respond to ongoing threats.

Tactical Threat Intelligence: This is the most granular form of threat intelligence, providing specific details about threats, such as indicators of compromise (IoCs), malware signatures, and IP addresses associated with malicious activity. It is crucial for identifying and mitigating immediate threats.

To leverage threat intelligence effectively, organizations need to establish robust processes for collecting, analyzing, and disseminating this information.

Many organizations subscribe to commercial threat intelligence services, which provide curated data and analysis about emerging threats.

These services aggregate information from a variety of sources, including open-source feeds, forums, and dark web forums, to provide timely and relevant threat intelligence.

In addition to commercial services, organizations can also benefit from sharing threat intelligence within industry-specific Information Sharing and Analysis Centers (ISACs) or through government-sponsored initiatives.

These collaborative efforts enable organizations to benefit from the collective knowledge of their peers and government agencies, further enhancing their ability to defend against threats.

When it comes to attribution, threat intelligence plays a critical role.

Attribution in cybersecurity refers to the process of identifying the individuals, groups, or nation-states responsible for a cyberattack.

While attribution can be challenging, threat intelligence can provide valuable clues.

For example, if a specific malware strain or attack method is associated with a known threat actor or group, this information can help attribute an attack to that entity.

Furthermore, indicators of compromise (IoCs) collected through threat intelligence can be used to trace an attack back to its source.

These IoCs may include IP addresses, domain names, or malware signatures associated with the attacker.

Advanced threat intelligence platforms use machine learning and artificial intelligence to analyze IoCs and other data to identify patterns and correlations that human analysts might miss.

This can significantly aid in the attribution process.

It's important to note that attribution is not always possible, especially when dealing with highly sophisticated threat actors who take measures to conceal their identities.

In such cases, threat intelligence can still provide valuable information about the tactics and motivations of the attacker, even if their identity remains unknown.

In addition to attribution, threat intelligence is invaluable for proactive defense.

Organizations can use threat intelligence to build and fine-tune their cybersecurity defenses.

For instance, if threat intelligence reveals a surge in phishing attacks using a specific type of lure, organizations can adjust their email filtering and employee training accordingly.

Similarly, if a new vulnerability is discovered in a widely used software application, threat intelligence can alert organizations to the potential risk and enable them to patch or mitigate the vulnerability before it's exploited.

By staying ahead of emerging threats, organizations can reduce their exposure to cyberattacks.

Collaboration is key in the world of threat intelligence.

Organizations must not only consume threat intelligence but also share their own findings and observations.

This collective effort helps create a more comprehensive and up-to-date understanding of the threat landscape.

Sharing threat intelligence with trusted partners, industry peers, and government agencies fosters a sense of community defense, where organizations work together to protect against common threats.

In summary, threat intelligence is a powerful tool in the arsenal of cybersecurity professionals.

It provides insights into the tactics, techniques, and motivations of cyber threat actors, helping organizations defend against emerging threats and, in some cases, attribute attacks to specific entities.

To leverage threat intelligence effectively, organizations must establish processes for collecting, analyzing, and sharing this valuable information.

By collaborating and staying informed, organizations can bolster their cybersecurity defenses and reduce their exposure to cyber threats in an ever-evolving digital landscape.

BOOK 4
EXPERT BLUE TEAM OPERATIONS
DEFENDING AGAINST ADVANCED THREATS

ROB BOTWRIGHT

Chapter 1: Advanced Threat Landscape Analysis

In the dynamic and constantly evolving field of cybersecurity, staying ahead of emerging threat actors and their evolving techniques is paramount for organizations and security professionals alike.

Threat actors, also known as malicious actors or adversaries, are the individuals, groups, or organizations responsible for carrying out cyberattacks with the intent to compromise, steal, disrupt, or damage digital assets and systems.

Emerging threat actors represent a diverse and ever-changing landscape that includes a wide range of actors, each with its own motivations and capabilities.

Understanding these threat actors and their tactics is crucial for effective cybersecurity defense.

One category of emerging threat actors includes nation-states or state-sponsored groups.

These threat actors often possess substantial resources, including advanced tools, significant financial backing, and highly skilled personnel.

Their motivations can vary widely, from espionage and data theft to political influence and sabotage.

State-sponsored threat actors are known for their ability to conduct sophisticated and stealthy operations, making attribution challenging.

Another category of emerging threat actors consists of cybercriminal organizations.

These groups operate with the primary goal of financial gain, engaging in activities like ransomware attacks, fraud, and identity theft.

They often use sophisticated techniques to infiltrate organizations and extract valuable data or demand ransoms.

Ransomware attacks, in particular, have gained notoriety for their disruptive and costly nature.

Hacktivists represent yet another category of emerging threat actors.

These individuals or groups are motivated by political, social, or ideological causes and use hacking as a means of protest or activism.

Hacktivists often target government agencies, corporations, or organizations they perceive as unethical or oppressive.

Their actions can lead to data breaches, defacement of websites, or distributed denial-of-service (DDoS) attacks.

Advanced Persistent Threat (APT) groups are a subset of emerging threat actors that warrant special attention.

APTs are typically state-sponsored or well-funded groups that conduct long-term, covert operations with specific strategic objectives.

They are known for their patience, precision, and ability to maintain persistence within targeted networks for extended periods.

APTs often employ a combination of zero-day exploits, custom malware, and social engineering techniques.

In addition to understanding the threat actors themselves, it's crucial to grasp the evolving techniques they employ.

One such technique is social engineering, which plays a significant role in many cyberattacks.

Social engineering involves manipulating individuals to divulge confidential information, click on malicious links, or perform actions that compromise security.

Phishing, spear-phishing, and pretexting are common social engineering tactics.

Ransomware attacks have also seen a rise in popularity among emerging threat actors.

These attacks involve encrypting an organization's data and demanding a ransom for its release.

Ransomware has evolved to become more targeted and destructive, with some variants even threatening to publish stolen data.

Supply chain attacks represent another concerning technique.

These attacks involve compromising a trusted supplier or vendor to gain access to a target organization's network.

Supply chain attacks can have widespread and far-reaching consequences.

As organizations adopt cloud computing and remote work solutions, threat actors have adapted their techniques accordingly.

Cloud-specific attacks, such as misconfigured cloud storage or identity and access management (IAM) abuse, have become more prevalent.

Zero-day exploits, which target vulnerabilities that are unknown to the software vendor, continue to be a favored tool among emerging threat actors.

These exploits can be highly effective because there are no available patches or defenses until the vulnerability is discovered and mitigated.

Spear-phishing, a more targeted form of phishing, is increasingly sophisticated.

Threat actors research their victims and craft convincing messages tailored to their interests and roles within organizations.

The use of machine learning and artificial intelligence (AI) in cyberattacks is an emerging trend.

Threat actors employ AI-driven techniques to automate attacks, making them more efficient and harder to detect.

In summary, understanding emerging threat actors and their evolving techniques is essential for effective cybersecurity.

Organizations and security professionals must stay vigilant, continuously update their defenses, and be prepared to respond to the ever-changing threat landscape.

This ongoing effort to adapt and defend against emerging threats is crucial for safeguarding digital assets, data, and the overall security of cyberspace.

Analyzing historical attack patterns is a valuable practice in the realm of cybersecurity, as it provides insights into the evolution of threats and the strategies employed by malicious actors over time. By examining these patterns, security professionals can better anticipate future attacks, enhance their defense mechanisms, and respond more effectively to emerging threats.

Historical attack patterns serve as a treasure trove of information, allowing us to trace the development of cyber threats from their nascent stages to their current sophistication. These patterns reveal a multitude of attack vectors and techniques that have been leveraged by threat actors throughout the history of cybersecurity.

One of the earliest attack patterns that gained prominence was the computer virus. In the 1980s, viruses like the Elk Cloner and Brain marked the beginning of malicious software spreading from one computer to another. These early viruses were relatively simple compared to today's sophisticated malware, but they set a precedent for future developments.

As personal computers became more prevalent, so did malware targeting them. The 1990s saw the rise of worms, which were capable of self-propagation through network vulnerabilities. The infamous "ILOVEYOU" worm in 2000 was a prominent example that infected millions of computers globally.

Phishing attacks, another historical attack pattern, have been a persistent threat since the early 2000s. These attacks involve luring victims into revealing sensitive information or installing malicious software through deceptive emails or websites. Over time, phishing techniques have become more convincing and targeted, making them a prevalent threat today.

Distributed Denial of Service (DDoS) attacks have also left their mark on the historical landscape of cyberattacks. The early 2000s saw the emergence of powerful botnets that could flood websites and servers with traffic, rendering them inaccessible. These attacks continue to evolve in scale and complexity, posing a significant challenge to organizations.

Historical attack patterns also include the exploitation of software vulnerabilities, commonly known as zero-day exploits. Threat actors have consistently leveraged unknown vulnerabilities to compromise systems, often leading to data breaches and system compromise. The development of exploits and their integration into malware has grown more sophisticated over time.

A notable historical attack pattern is the use of ransomware, which became prominent in the mid-2010s. Ransomware attacks involve encrypting a victim's data and demanding a ransom for its decryption. These attacks have evolved from generic campaigns to highly targeted and destructive operations, often causing significant financial losses.

Supply chain attacks, though not a new concept, have gained attention as a historical attack pattern due to their high-profile incidents. Threat actors target a trusted supplier or vendor to compromise the supply chain and gain access to the target organization's systems. The SolarWinds breach in 2020 exemplifies the severity of such attacks.

Historical attack patterns encompass not only the techniques used but also the motivations behind cyberattacks. Early motivations often revolved around curiosity and notoriety, with hackers seeking recognition for their skills. As the internet grew, financial gain became a primary motivator, leading to the proliferation of cybercriminal organizations.

Espionage and cyber-espionage have also played a significant role in historical attack patterns. Nation-states and state-sponsored threat actors have targeted governments, organizations, and critical infrastructure for political, economic, or strategic advantages. The Stuxnet worm, discovered in 2010, exemplified the potential impact of state-sponsored cyberattacks.

Over the years, hacktivism emerged as a motivation for cyberattacks. Hacktivist groups carry out attacks to advance social or political causes, often defacing websites, leaking sensitive information, or disrupting online services. The hacktivist collective Anonymous is one of the most well-known groups in this category.

Historical attack patterns demonstrate the adaptability of threat actors. As security measures improve, malicious actors develop new tactics to bypass defenses. The use of social engineering, spear-phishing, and targeted attacks has become more prevalent, emphasizing the need for user awareness and education.

Emerging technologies have introduced novel attack vectors. The Internet of Things (IoT), for instance, has opened new opportunities for attackers to target connected devices, potentially compromising privacy and security. As IoT adoption grows, so do the associated risks.

Analyzing historical attack patterns is not merely a retrospective exercise. It serves as a foundation for proactive cybersecurity. By understanding the evolution of threats and the tactics used by malicious actors, security professionals can better prepare for future challenges.

Security measures such as intrusion detection systems, threat intelligence sharing, and incident response protocols have evolved in response to historical attack patterns. Additionally, the cybersecurity community continuously researches and develops countermeasures to mitigate emerging threats.

In summary, the analysis of historical attack patterns is a crucial aspect of cybersecurity. It provides valuable insights into the evolution of cyber threats, the motivations behind attacks, and the techniques employed by threat actors. Armed with this knowledge, organizations and security professionals can better protect their systems and data from current and future cyber threats.

Chapter 2: Threat Intelligence Integration

Understanding the role of threat intelligence in defense is essential in today's cybersecurity landscape. Threat intelligence encompasses the collection, analysis, and dissemination of information about cyber threats, helping organizations make informed decisions to protect their systems and data.

In a world where cyber threats are ever-evolving, threat intelligence serves as a valuable asset for organizations striving to stay ahead of malicious actors. It empowers them with the knowledge needed to anticipate and respond to cyberattacks effectively.

At its core, threat intelligence provides organizations with situational awareness. It offers insights into the current threat landscape, including the tactics, techniques, and procedures employed by cybercriminals. This awareness enables organizations to identify potential vulnerabilities and proactively fortify their defenses.

Threat intelligence sources are diverse, ranging from open-source information to proprietary feeds and partnerships with security vendors. These sources provide valuable data about emerging threats, malware campaigns, vulnerabilities, and indicators of compromise.

One of the primary functions of threat intelligence is to detect and assess threats. By continuously monitoring for signs of malicious activity, organizations can detect potential security incidents in their early stages. This early detection is critical for minimizing the impact of an attack.

Threat intelligence also aids in understanding the motives and capabilities of threat actors. Whether they are financially motivated cybercriminals, hacktivists, or nation-state actors, knowing their objectives and capabilities is crucial for building effective defenses.

Furthermore, threat intelligence helps organizations prioritize their security efforts. Not all threats are equal, and organizations must allocate their resources wisely. Threat intelligence enables them to focus on the most relevant and imminent threats, thereby optimizing their security posture.

In addition to threat detection and prioritization, threat intelligence plays a significant role in incident response. When a security incident occurs, having relevant threat intelligence at hand can expedite the investigation and containment process. Analysts can correlate indicators of compromise with known threat intelligence to identify the nature of the attack and take appropriate action.

Beyond incident response, threat intelligence supports threat hunting. Threat hunters actively seek out signs of compromise within an organization's network, often using threat intelligence to guide their investigations. This proactive approach helps organizations identify threats that may have gone unnoticed by automated security systems.

Sharing threat intelligence is another critical aspect of its role in defense. Many organizations participate in information sharing and analysis centers (ISACs) or industry-specific information-sharing groups. These forums allow organizations to exchange threat intelligence with peers, enhancing collective security.

The role of threat intelligence extends to vulnerability management. It assists organizations in identifying vulnerabilities that threat actors may target. By addressing these vulnerabilities promptly, organizations can reduce their attack surface and minimize the risk of exploitation.

In addition to its tactical use in threat detection and response, threat intelligence has a strategic role in cybersecurity. It informs security leaders and executives about the broader cybersecurity landscape, enabling them to make informed decisions about security investments and policies.

Machine learning and artificial intelligence (AI) are increasingly being integrated into threat intelligence processes. These technologies can analyze vast amounts of data quickly, identifying patterns and anomalies that may indicate a threat. Machine learning models can also enhance the accuracy of threat detection.

The use of threat intelligence platforms (TIPs) has become common in organizations. TIPs streamline the collection, analysis, and dissemination of threat intelligence, making it more accessible and actionable for security teams.

To effectively harness the power of threat intelligence, organizations need a well-defined strategy. This strategy should outline how threat intelligence will be collected, analyzed, and integrated into security operations. It should also specify how threat intelligence will be shared with relevant stakeholders, both internally and externally.

In summary, the role of threat intelligence in defense is multifaceted and dynamic. It serves as a critical component of modern cybersecurity, providing organizations with the insights and knowledge needed to protect against a wide range of cyber threats. As the threat landscape continues to evolve, threat intelligence will remain an indispensable tool for organizations striving to secure their digital assets and data.

Implementing threat intelligence sharing frameworks is a crucial step for organizations seeking to bolster their cybersecurity defenses. These frameworks facilitate the exchange of threat intelligence between organizations, enabling them to collectively respond to and mitigate cyber threats.

The need for threat intelligence sharing has become increasingly evident in today's interconnected digital landscape. Cyber threats often transcend organizational boundaries, and no single entity can combat them effectively in isolation. Threat actors are known to target multiple organizations simultaneously, exploiting similar vulnerabilities and attack vectors.

By sharing threat intelligence, organizations can pool their knowledge and resources to detect and respond to threats more efficiently. This collaborative approach strengthens the overall security posture of participating entities and enhances the cybersecurity ecosystem as a whole.

One commonly used framework for threat intelligence sharing is Information Sharing and Analysis Centers (ISACs). ISACs are industry-specific organizations that facilitate the exchange of threat intelligence among members within a particular sector, such as finance, healthcare, or energy.

ISACs serve as trusted intermediaries, providing a secure platform for members to share sensitive threat information without exposing proprietary or confidential data. They enable organizations to contribute indicators of compromise (IOCs), threat actor tactics, and other relevant information to a collective pool.

To implement an ISAC-based threat intelligence sharing framework, organizations typically join an established ISAC relevant to their industry. Once a member, they gain access to a community of peers who share similar cybersecurity concerns.

Participation in an ISAC requires a commitment to contribute and consume threat intelligence actively. Organizations should be willing to share relevant threat data while also benefiting from the shared insights of other members.

Another framework for threat intelligence sharing is the Structured Threat Information eXpression (STIX) and Trusted Automated Exchange of Indicator Information (TAXII). These standards are developed and maintained by the Cyber Threat Intelligence Technical Committee (CTI TC) of the Organization for the Advancement of Structured Information Standards (OASIS).

STIX is a standardized language for representing and exchanging cyber threat intelligence. It provides a common format for encoding information about threats, incidents, vulnerabilities, and other cybersecurity-related data. STIX enables organizations to express complex threat information in a structured and machine-readable format.

TAXII, on the other hand, is a protocol that facilitates the automated exchange of cyber threat information. It enables organizations to share threat intelligence data in a timely and efficient manner. TAXII defines a set of services and message exchanges for securely transmitting threat information between parties.

Implementing STIX and TAXII-based threat intelligence sharing involves adopting these standards within an organization's cybersecurity infrastructure. This may require integration with existing security tools and platforms to ensure seamless data exchange.

Open-source threat intelligence sharing platforms, such as MISP (Malware Information Sharing Platform & Threat Sharing), also play a crucial role in enabling organizations to share threat information. MISP is designed to support the sharing of structured threat information, including indicators, threat actor profiles, and attack patterns.

Organizations can deploy MISP within their environments, allowing them to collect, store, and disseminate threat intelligence. MISP instances can be interconnected to form a global network of information sharing, enabling organizations to collaborate with others worldwide.

When implementing threat intelligence sharing frameworks, organizations should consider several key factors. First and foremost, they must define their objectives and goals for sharing threat intelligence. These objectives may include improving threat detection, enhancing incident response, or increasing situational awareness.

Organizations should also assess the legal and regulatory considerations associated with sharing threat intelligence. Compliance with data protection laws and regulations is paramount when sharing sensitive information with external parties.

Furthermore, organizations must establish clear policies and procedures for sharing threat intelligence. These policies should address issues such as data classification, information sharing agreements, and incident reporting processes.

To ensure the security of shared threat intelligence, organizations should employ encryption and access controls to protect sensitive data. It is essential to establish trust relationships with sharing partners and implement mechanisms for secure communication.

Additionally, organizations should continuously evaluate the effectiveness of their threat intelligence sharing initiatives. Metrics and key performance indicators (KPIs) can help assess the impact of sharing on security outcomes.

In summary, implementing threat intelligence sharing frameworks is a strategic imperative for organizations seeking to enhance their cybersecurity resilience. By collaborating with peers, leveraging standards like STIX and TAXII, and participating in ISACs and open-source platforms like MISP, organizations can tap into a broader pool of threat intelligence and strengthen their defenses against cyber threats. With clear objectives, policies, and security measures in place, threat intelligence sharing can become a cornerstone of effective cybersecurity practices in today's dynamic threat landscape.

Chapter 3: Advanced Network Defense Strategies

Next-generation firewall (NGFW) and intrusion prevention systems (IPS) represent significant advancements in network security, providing organizations with robust defenses against a wide range of cyber threats.

NGFWs are a natural evolution of traditional firewalls, designed to address the limitations of older security technologies. They combine traditional firewall capabilities with additional features such as application-layer filtering, deep packet inspection, and threat intelligence integration.

The core functionality of an NGFW remains firewalling, where it controls incoming and outgoing network traffic based on a set of predetermined security rules. However, unlike traditional firewalls that primarily rely on port and protocol information, NGFWs inspect traffic at a deeper level, examining the actual content and context of packets.

One of the key features of NGFWs is the ability to identify and control applications running on the network. This application awareness allows organizations to implement granular access policies based on specific applications or application categories. For example, an NGFW can allow or block access to social media, file-sharing, or gaming applications, helping organizations enforce security and compliance policies.

Deep packet inspection (DPI) is another critical component of NGFWs. DPI enables the examination of packet contents and metadata to identify and block malicious traffic. This capability is particularly effective in detecting and preventing advanced threats that may be concealed within seemingly legitimate traffic.

Intrusion prevention systems (IPS) work in tandem with NGFWs to provide real-time threat detection and prevention. IPS solutions are designed to identify and block known and unknown threats by inspecting network traffic for suspicious patterns or signatures.

IPS solutions employ a combination of signature-based and behavior-based analysis techniques. Signature-based detection involves comparing network traffic to a database of known attack patterns or signatures. If a match is found, the IPS takes immediate action to block the threat.

Behavior-based detection, on the other hand, focuses on analyzing the behavior of network traffic. This approach looks for deviations from normal traffic patterns and can detect previously unseen or zero-day attacks. When suspicious behavior is identified, the IPS can trigger an alert or take preventive measures.

Integration with threat intelligence feeds is a crucial aspect of both NGFWs and IPS solutions. Threat intelligence provides these systems with up-to-date information about emerging threats, known attack sources, and malicious IP addresses. By leveraging threat intelligence, NGFWs and IPS solutions can proactively block threats, even before they are formally identified and added to signature databases.

Another important feature of NGFWs and IPS is their ability to support secure remote access through virtual private network (VPN) capabilities. VPNs enable remote users to connect securely to an organization's network over the internet, ensuring that sensitive data remains protected during transit.

Furthermore, NGFWs and IPS solutions often incorporate intrusion detection system (IDS) functionality. IDSs passively monitor network traffic, analyzing it for signs of suspicious activity without taking direct action. When an IDS detects a potential threat, it generates an alert for further investigation by security personnel.

Effective management and centralized control are essential for deploying NGFWs and IPS solutions in complex network environments. Organizations often employ security information and event management (SIEM) systems to consolidate and analyze data from NGFWs, IPS devices, and other security tools. SIEM platforms enable security teams to correlate events, identify potential threats, and respond promptly to security incidents.

While NGFWs and IPS solutions offer significant advantages in terms of security, they are not without challenges. Organizations must carefully configure these systems to avoid false positives and negatives, ensuring that legitimate traffic is not mistakenly blocked while threats are effectively mitigated.

Additionally, NGFWs and IPS solutions require ongoing updates to their threat intelligence feeds and signatures to remain effective against evolving threats. Regular maintenance and monitoring are essential to keep these security measures up to date and responsive to the latest cybersecurity threats.

In summary, next-generation firewalls (NGFWs) and intrusion prevention systems (IPS) play a vital role in modern network security. They offer advanced capabilities such as application awareness, deep packet inspection, and threat intelligence integration, enabling organizations to protect their networks against a wide range of cyber threats. When combined with effective management, monitoring, and ongoing updates, NGFWs and IPS solutions provide a robust defense against the ever-changing landscape of cybersecurity threats.

Network segmentation and the zero trust architecture are

two critical components of modern cybersecurity strategies that work together to enhance network security and protect against evolving cyber threats.

Network segmentation is the practice of dividing a network into smaller, isolated segments or subnetworks to improve security and reduce the attack surface. Each segment typically contains a specific set of resources, such as servers, workstations, or IoT devices, and has its own security policies and controls.

The primary goal of network segmentation is to limit lateral movement for attackers within a network. By separating resources into different segments, even if one segment is compromised, the attacker's ability to move laterally to other segments is restricted, limiting the overall impact of a breach.

For example, a common segmentation practice is to separate the corporate network from the guest network. This ensures that guests and external devices have limited access to internal resources, reducing the risk of unauthorized access to sensitive data or systems.

Zero trust architecture, on the other hand, is a security model that assumes no implicit trust, even among users or devices inside a network. In a zero trust environment, access to resources is granted based on strict identity verification and continuous monitoring of user and device behavior.

The core principles of zero trust include:

Verify identity: Users and devices must authenticate themselves before gaining access to resources. This often involves multi-factor authentication (MFA) and strong authentication methods.

Least privilege access: Users and devices are granted the minimum level of access required to perform their tasks. This principle helps reduce the attack surface by limiting unnecessary access rights.

Micro-segmentation: Zero trust networks are further divided into micro-segments, where specific policies are applied to individual resources or applications. This fine-grained control enhances security.

Continuous monitoring: User and device behavior is continuously monitored for suspicious activity. Any deviations from normal behavior can trigger alerts or access restrictions.

Data encryption: Data should be encrypted both in transit and at rest to protect it from unauthorized access, even within the network.

When combined, network segmentation and zero trust architecture provide a robust defense against cyber threats. Network segmentation creates distinct security zones within a network, reducing the potential impact of a breach, while zero trust ensures that all network traffic is subject to rigorous authentication and authorization checks.

Implementing network segmentation can be achieved through various methods, including the use of firewalls, virtual LANs (VLANs), and access control lists (ACLs). These tools enable organizations to define policies that control traffic flow between segments and enforce security rules.

Zero trust architecture, on the other hand, involves deploying identity and access management (IAM) solutions, implementing strong authentication mechanisms, and continuously monitoring user and device behavior. This approach requires a shift in mindset, moving from the traditional perimeter-based security model to one that places security at the core of every network interaction.

A key advantage of network segmentation and zero trust architecture is their adaptability to dynamic environments. As networks evolve, segments can be added or modified to accommodate changes in business needs, and access policies can be adjusted accordingly. This flexibility is crucial in today's fast-paced digital landscape.

Moreover, the integration of network segmentation and zero trust can help organizations address specific cybersecurity challenges, such as:

Insider threats: By implementing zero trust principles, even authorized users are subject to stringent access controls and monitoring, reducing the risk of insider threats.

Remote work: In an era of remote work, where employees access resources from various locations and devices, zero trust ensures that access is secure, regardless of the user's location.

Cloud adoption: As organizations migrate to cloud environments, network segmentation and zero trust can protect cloud-based resources and data from unauthorized access.

Third-party access: When third-party vendors or partners require access to an organization's network, network segmentation and zero trust principles can be applied to limit their access to specific resources.

Compliance requirements: Many regulatory frameworks mandate strong access controls and data protection measures. Network segmentation and zero trust can help organizations meet these compliance requirements.

To implement network segmentation and zero trust effectively, organizations must undergo a comprehensive planning and assessment phase. This involves identifying critical assets, defining access policies, and establishing monitoring and response procedures.

Additionally, ongoing maintenance and monitoring are essential to ensure that network segmentation and zero trust controls remain effective over time. Regular assessments and updates are necessary to adapt to changing threats and business requirements.

In summary, network segmentation and zero trust architecture are integral components of modern cybersecurity strategies. Network segmentation creates security zones within a network, limiting the potential impact of breaches, while zero trust ensures that all network interactions are subject to strict identity verification and continuous monitoring. By implementing these practices together, organizations can strengthen their defenses against a wide range of cyber threats and adapt to evolving security challenges in today's digital landscape.

Chapter 4: Endpoint Security and Advanced Threat Detection

In the ever-evolving landscape of cybersecurity, advanced endpoint protection solutions have become indispensable for safeguarding organizations against a multitude of threats and attacks. These solutions, often referred to as advanced endpoint security or endpoint detection and response (EDR) solutions, are designed to provide comprehensive defense mechanisms at the endpoint level.

At their core, advanced endpoint protection solutions focus on protecting individual devices, such as laptops, desktops, servers, and mobile devices, from a wide array of threats, including malware, ransomware, zero-day exploits, and sophisticated attacks.

One of the key features of advanced endpoint protection is real-time threat detection and response. These solutions employ advanced algorithms and artificial intelligence (AI) to continuously monitor endpoint activity, looking for suspicious or malicious behavior. When such behavior is detected, the solution can take immediate action to mitigate the threat, such as isolating the infected device from the network or rolling back changes made by malware.

A critical aspect of advanced endpoint protection is its ability to provide visibility into the endpoint environment. This visibility allows security teams to gain insights into the state of their endpoints, including the presence of vulnerabilities, unauthorized software, and potentially malicious processes. Armed with this information, organizations can make informed decisions to improve their security posture.

Another significant feature of advanced endpoint protection is its ability to investigate incidents retroactively. Security professionals can use EDR solutions to conduct forensic analysis of past incidents, helping them understand how a threat entered the network, moved laterally, and exfiltrated data. This retrospective analysis is invaluable for improving security strategies and preventing future attacks.

Moreover, these solutions often include threat hunting capabilities, which allow security analysts to proactively search for threats and vulnerabilities within their network. By taking a proactive approach to threat hunting, organizations can identify and neutralize potential threats before they can cause harm.

One of the key challenges in modern cybersecurity is the rapidly evolving nature of threats. Traditional antivirus software is often unable to keep up with new and sophisticated attacks. Advanced endpoint protection solutions address this challenge by using AI and machine learning to detect previously unknown threats.

These solutions build a baseline of "normal" behavior for each endpoint and raise alerts when deviations from this baseline occur. This behavior-based approach is effective at identifying zero-day attacks and other advanced threats that evade signature-based detection.

In addition to real-time threat detection and behavior analysis, advanced endpoint protection solutions typically include features like threat intelligence integration. This means they can leverage threat intelligence feeds to stay updated on the latest threats and indicators of compromise (IOCs).

By incorporating threat intelligence into their defenses, organizations can proactively protect their endpoints against known threats and indicators. This is especially crucial when facing threats like advanced persistent threats (APTs) and nation-state-sponsored attacks.

Furthermore, advanced endpoint protection solutions often offer containment and remediation capabilities. When a threat is detected, these solutions can isolate the infected endpoint from the network, preventing lateral movement and further damage. After containment, they can initiate automated or manual remediation processes to eliminate the threat.

Endpoint protection also plays a crucial role in the overall security of an organization. Endpoints are often the entry point for attackers, and a compromised device can provide attackers with a foothold within the network. Therefore, securing endpoints is a critical aspect of a layered security strategy.

Endpoint protection solutions are designed to complement other security measures, such as firewalls, intrusion detection systems, and email filtering. They serve as the last line of defense, ensuring that even if threats manage to bypass other security layers, they are still detected and stopped at the endpoint.

In addition to protecting against external threats, advanced endpoint protection solutions are essential for addressing insider threats. These solutions can monitor and audit user and system activity, helping organizations detect and respond to malicious actions or policy violations by employees or other insiders.

When considering advanced endpoint protection solutions, organizations should take into account factors such as ease of deployment, scalability, and integration with existing security infrastructure. The ability to manage and monitor endpoints from a centralized console is also a crucial consideration.

Furthermore, organizations must ensure that their chosen solution is compliant with regulatory requirements and can generate the necessary reports and logs for auditing purposes. Compliance with regulations such as GDPR, HIPAA, and PCI DSS is essential for organizations in various industries.

Endpoint protection is not a one-size-fits-all solution. Different organizations have varying needs and risk profiles. Therefore, it's essential to select an advanced endpoint protection solution that aligns with an organization's specific requirements.

To maximize the effectiveness of advanced endpoint protection solutions, organizations should also invest in employee training and security awareness programs. Human error remains a significant contributor to security incidents, and educating employees on best practices for endpoint security can help mitigate this risk.

In summary, advanced endpoint protection solutions have become indispensable in the modern cybersecurity landscape. These solutions provide real-time threat detection, behavior analysis, retrospective incident investigation, and threat hunting capabilities. By leveraging AI, machine learning, and threat intelligence, they offer robust defense against a wide range of threats, including zero-day attacks. Endpoint protection is a critical component of a layered security strategy and plays a crucial role in safeguarding organizations against external and insider threats. When selecting an endpoint protection solution, organizations should consider factors such as ease of deployment, scalability, compliance, and integration with existing security infrastructure. Furthermore, employee training and security awareness programs should complement endpoint protection measures to create a comprehensive security posture.

Machine learning and artificial intelligence (AI) have emerged as powerful tools in the realm of threat detection, revolutionizing the way cybersecurity professionals defend against a myriad of digital threats. These technologies, once confined to the realm of science fiction, have found real-world application in identifying and mitigating security risks with remarkable accuracy and efficiency.

At the heart of machine learning and AI in threat detection lies the ability to analyze vast amounts of data at speeds no human could match. Traditional methods of threat detection often rely on static signatures and known patterns to identify malicious activity. While effective to a certain extent, these approaches fall short in the face of rapidly evolving threats.

Machine learning and AI, on the other hand, excel at recognizing subtle, previously unseen patterns and anomalies within the data. They do this by leveraging algorithms that can adapt and improve their accuracy over time, making them ideally suited to detect emerging and sophisticated threats.

One of the key advantages of machine learning and AI in threat detection is their ability to reduce false positives. False positives, or erroneous alerts that indicate a threat where none exists, can overwhelm cybersecurity teams and lead to alert fatigue. Machine learning models can learn from historical data to differentiate between genuine threats and benign events, thus minimizing false alarms.

An important application of machine learning in threat detection is the use of supervised learning models. In supervised learning, models are trained on labeled datasets, which means they are provided with examples of both malicious and benign data. These models learn to distinguish between the two categories, enabling them to identify similar patterns in new, unseen data.

Unsupervised learning is another valuable technique in threat detection. Unlike supervised learning, unsupervised models are not provided with labeled data. Instead, they identify patterns and anomalies within the data on their own, making them highly adaptable to emerging threats that may not have been seen before.

Reinforcement learning, a subset of machine learning, is also gaining traction in threat detection. In reinforcement learning, models learn by interacting with their environment and receiving feedback in the form of rewards or penalties. This approach can be used to create autonomous agents that make real-time decisions in response to threats.

Natural language processing (NLP) is yet another area where machine learning is making significant inroads in cybersecurity. NLP algorithms can analyze and understand human language, which is crucial for threat detection in areas such as email security. By examining the content of emails and messages, NLP models can identify phishing attempts, malware-laden attachments, and other forms of malicious communication.

Machine learning models are also used for anomaly detection, a critical aspect of threat detection. Anomaly detection involves identifying deviations from expected behavior within a system or network. For example, an AI-powered intrusion detection system can continuously monitor network traffic and flag any unusual patterns or behaviors that may indicate a security breach.

AI-driven threat detection is not limited to network security. It extends to endpoint security as well, where machine learning models can analyze the behavior of individual devices and endpoints to detect signs of compromise. This approach allows organizations to protect their endpoints against a wide range of threats, including malware, ransomware, and zero-day exploits.

The integration of machine learning and AI in threat detection is not without its challenges. These technologies require substantial computing power and large datasets for training, which may pose resource constraints for some organizations. Additionally, the potential for adversarial attacks, where threat actors attempt to deceive machine learning models, is a growing concern.

Despite these challenges, the benefits of incorporating machine learning and AI into threat detection are undeniable. These technologies have the potential to stay ahead of evolving threats, reduce false positives, and provide cybersecurity professionals with the tools they need to defend against increasingly sophisticated attacks.

Moreover, machine learning and AI have the capacity to automate many aspects of threat detection and response, allowing cybersecurity teams to focus their efforts on higher-level tasks and strategic planning. For example, AI-powered security orchestration and automation platforms can streamline incident response by automatically containing threats, isolating compromised devices, and initiating remediation actions.

In the realm of threat intelligence, machine learning and AI can enhance the analysis of vast amounts of data from multiple sources, providing security professionals with actionable insights into emerging threats and attack trends. These technologies can help organizations make data-driven decisions and prioritize security measures accordingly.

It's important to note that machine learning and AI are not a panacea for all cybersecurity challenges. They should be seen as complementary tools that work alongside traditional security measures, such as firewalls, antivirus software, and intrusion detection systems. A multi-layered security approach that combines these technologies can provide organizations with a robust defense against a wide range of threats.

Furthermore, the field of machine learning and AI in cybersecurity is continuously evolving. Researchers and security practitioners are continually developing new techniques and models to stay ahead of the threat landscape. As threats become more sophisticated, the cybersecurity community must adapt and innovate to keep pace.

In summary, machine learning and artificial intelligence have ushered in a new era of threat detection in cybersecurity. These technologies excel at analyzing vast amounts of data, recognizing subtle patterns, and reducing false positives. They have applications in supervised and unsupervised learning, reinforcement learning, natural language processing, and anomaly detection. Machine learning and AI are invaluable tools for staying ahead of evolving threats, automating threat detection and response, and gaining insights from threat intelligence. While challenges exist, these technologies represent a significant advancement in the ongoing battle against cyber threats.

Chapter 5: Behavioral Analysis and Anomaly Detection

Behavioral profiling is a cutting-edge approach in the field of threat detection, offering a dynamic and adaptable strategy to identify and mitigate cybersecurity threats. It's a departure from traditional signature-based methods that rely on known patterns or indicators of compromise.

At its core, behavioral profiling involves monitoring the behavior of users, systems, and networks to establish a baseline of normal activity. This baseline serves as a reference point for identifying deviations that may indicate malicious activity.

Unlike static signatures that can become obsolete as threats evolve, behavioral profiling has the advantage of adaptability. It can detect both known threats and emerging ones by focusing on anomalous behavior rather than relying on predefined patterns.

Behavioral profiling leverages the power of machine learning and artificial intelligence to analyze vast datasets and identify subtle deviations from established norms. These technologies excel at recognizing patterns that may be indicative of a security breach, even when those patterns are not explicitly defined.

For instance, consider an organization's network traffic. Behavioral profiling systems can analyze historical network data to understand the typical communication patterns between devices. This may include the types of protocols used, the volume of data transferred, and the timing of communications.

Once a baseline is established, the system continuously monitors network traffic in real-time. If it detects deviations, such as unusual data transfer volumes, unexpected communication patterns, or unauthorized access attempts, it can trigger alerts for further investigation.

User behavior is another crucial aspect of behavioral profiling. It involves monitoring how users interact with IT systems and applications. Behavioral profiling systems can learn the typical behavior of each user, including their login times, the systems they access, and their typical data access patterns.

When a user's behavior deviates from their established baseline, it can trigger an alert. For example, if a user who typically accesses certain files or applications suddenly attempts to access sensitive data they've never interacted with before, the system can flag this behavior as suspicious.

Endpoint behavior is also a prime focus of behavioral profiling. By analyzing how endpoints (computers, servers, mobile devices, etc.) interact with the network and applications, behavioral profiling can identify unusual activities, such as a device connecting to an unfamiliar server or running unauthorized processes.

The beauty of behavioral profiling is that it adapts to the unique characteristics of each organization. It recognizes that what is normal for one organization may not be normal for another. This adaptability makes it particularly effective in detecting insider threats, where malicious activity may mimic normal behavior to evade detection.

Furthermore, behavioral profiling can help organizations prioritize alerts and incidents. By assigning risk scores to detected anomalies, it can help security teams focus their attention on the most significant threats rather than overwhelming them with a high volume of alerts.

To implement behavioral profiling effectively, organizations must invest in robust security information and event management (SIEM) systems, which provide the necessary data collection and analysis capabilities. SIEM platforms collect data from various sources, including network devices, servers, and endpoints, and use machine learning algorithms to identify suspicious behavior.

It's important to note that while behavioral profiling is a powerful tool, it should not be used in isolation. A comprehensive cybersecurity strategy should combine multiple layers of security, including firewalls, antivirus software, intrusion detection systems, and incident response plans.

Behavioral profiling also requires careful tuning and customization to avoid false positives. An overly sensitive system may trigger frequent alerts for benign behavior, leading to alert fatigue among security teams. Therefore, organizations must strike a balance between sensitivity and accuracy.

Moreover, organizations should consider privacy concerns when implementing behavioral profiling. Monitoring user behavior raises questions about privacy and data protection. It's essential to establish clear policies and communicate transparently with employees about the purpose and scope of monitoring.

In summary, behavioral profiling is a powerful approach to threat detection that focuses on identifying anomalies in user, system, and network behavior. It leverages the capabilities of machine learning and artificial intelligence to establish baselines of normal activity and detect deviations that may indicate security threats. By adapting to the unique characteristics of each organization, behavioral profiling offers an effective way to detect both known and emerging threats. However, it should be part of a broader cybersecurity strategy that includes other security measures and safeguards privacy considerations.

In the realm of cybersecurity, anomaly detection models and algorithms play a pivotal role in safeguarding systems and networks from threats. These models are designed to identify unusual patterns or deviations from the norm that may indicate potential security breaches or malicious activities.

At its core, anomaly detection is all about recognizing what is abnormal within a given context. This involves analyzing vast amounts of data, such as network traffic, user behavior, or system events, and identifying instances that stand out as atypical. The assumption here is that most of the data reflects normal, legitimate activities, while anomalies may indicate security incidents.

One common use case for anomaly detection is in network security. By continuously monitoring network traffic and comparing it to established baselines, these models can detect unusual patterns that may signify an ongoing attack. For example, a sudden surge in data transfer or repeated access attempts to a particular server may trigger an alert.

To build effective anomaly detection models, machine learning techniques are often employed. These techniques leverage historical data to train the model and establish what constitutes normal behavior. Once trained, the model can then identify deviations from this norm. One popular approach is the use of unsupervised learning algorithms, where the model learns patterns without being explicitly provided with labeled data.

Cluster-based anomaly detection is a widely used technique in this domain. It involves grouping data points into clusters based on similarity. Data points that do not fit well within any cluster are considered anomalies. For instance, in network traffic analysis, normal network behavior may form distinct clusters, while anomalies represent data points outside these clusters.

Another approach is statistical anomaly detection, which relies on probability and statistical models. By analyzing the distribution of data and calculating probabilities, this method can flag data points that fall outside expected ranges. For example, if user login times follow a specific statistical distribution, any deviations from this distribution may be flagged as anomalies.

Time series analysis is particularly important in anomaly detection, as it allows models to consider how data changes over time. In cybersecurity, the timing of events can be critical in identifying threats. By analyzing the time sequences of data points, models can spot anomalies that occur at unusual times or with unusual frequencies.

Machine learning algorithms like Isolation Forests, One-Class SVM, and autoencoders have gained popularity for their effectiveness in anomaly detection. Isolation Forests create partitions in the data to isolate anomalies, making them easier to detect. One-Class SVMs aim to find a hyperplane that separates normal data from anomalies. Autoencoders are neural networks trained to encode and decode data, making them adept at identifying irregularities.

Deep learning techniques, such as recurrent neural networks (RNNs) and convolutional neural networks (CNNs), have also shown promise in anomaly detection. RNNs are particularly well-suited for time series data, as they can capture sequential dependencies. CNNs excel at identifying spatial patterns in data, making them useful in image-based anomaly detection.

One crucial aspect of anomaly detection is tuning the models to strike a balance between sensitivity and specificity. Overly sensitive models may generate many false positives, causing alert fatigue among security teams. Conversely, models that are too specific may miss genuine threats. Thus, finding the right threshold for triggering alerts is a crucial part of implementing anomaly detection effectively.

Additionally, anomaly detection models must adapt to changing conditions and emerging threats. Threat actors continually evolve their tactics, and models must be updated to recognize new anomalies. Continuous monitoring and regular retraining of models are essential to keep up with the evolving threat landscape.

Anomaly detection is not limited to network security but extends to various domains, including fraud detection, industrial process monitoring, and healthcare. In each case, the goal is to spot unusual patterns or outliers that may indicate problems or security breaches.

As organizations increasingly rely on automation and AI-driven solutions, anomaly detection models will continue to play a vital role in proactively identifying and mitigating cybersecurity threats. These models, when integrated with other security measures, form a robust defense against a wide range of threats, from malware and phishing attacks to insider threats and zero-day vulnerabilities.

In summary, anomaly detection models and algorithms are critical tools in cybersecurity, helping organizations identify unusual patterns or deviations from the norm that may indicate security threats or breaches. Leveraging machine learning and statistical techniques, these models analyze vast amounts of data to spot anomalies, and they play a pivotal role in network security, fraud detection, and other domains. However, finding the right balance between sensitivity and specificity and ensuring continuous adaptation to emerging threats are key challenges in implementing effective anomaly detection systems.

Chapter 6: Advanced Incident Response Tactics

In the ever-evolving landscape of cybersecurity, threat hunting has emerged as a proactive approach to identifying and mitigating security threats that may go undetected by traditional security measures. Unlike traditional cybersecurity measures that primarily focus on detecting known threats or vulnerabilities, threat hunting involves actively searching for signs of suspicious or malicious activities within an organization's network and systems.

At its core, threat hunting is a detective process, akin to a digital detective or investigator, where cybersecurity experts or threat hunters use their knowledge, skills, and a variety of tools to look for subtle indicators of compromise or unusual patterns in the organization's data and network traffic. The goal is to find potential threats before they escalate into full-fledged security incidents.

One of the fundamental principles of threat hunting is the assumption that determined and skilled threat actors can evade traditional security measures, such as firewalls and antivirus software. These adversaries are often referred to as advanced persistent threats (APTs) and employ sophisticated techniques to stay hidden within a network, making them challenging to detect.

To effectively hunt for threats, organizations often establish dedicated threat hunting teams or leverage the expertise of experienced cybersecurity professionals. These experts possess an in-depth understanding of the organization's network architecture, applications, and typical user behavior, which helps them differentiate between normal and potentially malicious activities.

One of the key techniques employed in threat hunting is the use of threat intelligence. Threat intelligence provides valuable information about known threats, attack techniques, and the tactics, techniques, and procedures (TTPs) of threat actors. Threat hunters use this intelligence to create hypotheses about potential threats and then investigate those hypotheses within the organization's environment.

Hunting for threats involves analyzing various sources of data, including network traffic logs, system logs, endpoint telemetry, and even external threat intelligence feeds. The goal is to identify anomalies or suspicious patterns that could indicate a security threat. For instance, an unexpected surge in outbound network traffic or unusual login behavior may be signs of a potential breach.

Threat hunters also rely on behavioral analytics and machine learning algorithms to assist in their investigations. These tools can help identify patterns of behavior that deviate from the norm, potentially flagging unusual activities that require further investigation.

In addition to hunting for existing threats, threat hunters also engage in threat anticipation. This proactive approach involves considering hypothetical threat scenarios and assessing the organization's readiness to detect and respond to such threats. By doing so, organizations can better prepare for emerging threats and strengthen their security posture.

An essential aspect of threat hunting is the continuous improvement of detection techniques. Threat hunters learn from each investigation and refine their methods to become more effective over time. This iterative process is crucial in an environment where threat actors constantly evolve their tactics.

To be successful, threat hunting requires a collaborative and multidisciplinary approach. It involves close coordination between threat hunters, incident responders, and security analysts. When a potential threat is identified, threat hunters work alongside incident responders to assess the severity of the threat, contain it, and remediate any damage.

Threat hunting also aligns with the concept of zero trust security, which assumes that threats can exist both inside and outside the network. Therefore, organizations adopting zero trust principles often incorporate threat hunting as a proactive measure to continuously validate the security of their systems and data.

While threat hunting can be resource-intensive, the investment can pay off by identifying threats early in their lifecycle, minimizing potential damage, and reducing the overall impact of security incidents. It is an essential component of a mature cybersecurity strategy, complementing traditional security measures such as firewalls, intrusion detection systems, and antivirus software.

In summary, threat hunting is a proactive approach to cybersecurity that involves actively searching for signs of suspicious or malicious activities within an organization's network and systems. It is a detective process that relies on the expertise of cybersecurity professionals, threat intelligence, data analysis, and behavioral analytics. Threat hunters play a critical role in identifying and mitigating security threats that may go undetected by traditional security measures. As threats continue to evolve, threat hunting remains a valuable tool for organizations to bolster their security defenses and stay ahead of adversaries.

In the world of cybersecurity, incident containment and rapid response are critical components of an organization's defense strategy. When a security incident occurs, time is of the essence, and the ability to contain the incident swiftly can make all the difference in minimizing damage and reducing the impact on the organization.

To understand the significance of incident containment and rapid response, it's essential to recognize that no organization is entirely immune to security incidents. Whether it's a data breach, a malware infection, a denial-of-service attack, or any other form of cyberattack, the key is how effectively an organization can identify and contain the incident when it happens.

Incident containment refers to the actions taken to prevent a security incident from spreading further within an organization's network or affecting more systems and data. The primary goal is to isolate the incident to a limited scope, thereby limiting the attacker's access and minimizing potential damage.

Rapid response, on the other hand, pertains to the speed and efficiency with which an organization can react to a security incident once it has been detected. This involves not only containing the incident but also investigating it, understanding the nature of the attack, and formulating a plan for mitigation and recovery.

One of the fundamental principles of incident containment and rapid response is having a well-defined incident response plan in place. This plan serves as a playbook for how the organization will react when a security incident occurs. It outlines roles and responsibilities, communication protocols, and a series of predefined steps to be taken in the event of an incident. Key elements of an incident response plan include the establishment of an incident response team (IRT) composed of individuals with the necessary skills and expertise to handle security incidents. The team should include incident responders, forensic experts, legal counsel, and communication specialists, among others. When an incident is detected, the incident response team must swing into action promptly. This typically involves the following steps:

Identification: Recognizing that an incident has occurred, which may involve monitoring alerts, analyzing logs, or receiving reports from end-users.

Containment: Taking immediate steps to limit the impact of the incident. This might involve isolating affected systems, disconnecting from the network, or blocking malicious traffic.

Eradication: Identifying the root cause of the incident and eliminating it. This could include removing malware, closing vulnerabilities, or patching systems.

Recovery: Restoring affected systems and services to normal operation. This step is crucial to minimize downtime and disruptions.

Lessons Learned: After the incident has been contained and resolved, conducting a thorough post-incident review to assess what went well and where improvements can be made. A critical aspect of rapid response is the utilization of technology and tools that aid in the detection and containment of incidents. Intrusion detection systems (IDS), intrusion prevention systems (IPS), security information and event management (SIEM) solutions, and endpoint detection and response (EDR) tools play vital roles in this regard.

Moreover, automation and orchestration can significantly enhance the speed of incident response. Automated incident response workflows can execute predefined actions based on the type and severity of an incident, reducing the time it takes to contain and mitigate threats. Incident containment and rapid response also involve a strong focus on communication, both within the incident response team and with external stakeholders. Effective communication ensures that everyone is on the same page, from the technical experts working to contain the incident to senior management and legal teams handling public relations and legal obligations.

In today's interconnected and data-driven world, organizations must be prepared for a wide range of security incidents. These can include everything from external cyberattacks to insider threats, accidental data leaks, and even natural disasters affecting data centers. The ability to swiftly contain and respond to these incidents is a fundamental aspect of any robust cybersecurity strategy.

Furthermore, compliance requirements and regulations often mandate that organizations have incident response plans in place. Failing to comply with these requirements can result in severe penalties and reputational damage. Therefore, incident containment and rapid response are not just best practices but legal obligations in many industries.

It's worth noting that the cybersecurity landscape is continually evolving. Threat actors become more sophisticated, and new attack vectors emerge regularly. As a result, incident containment and rapid response strategies must also evolve and adapt to keep pace with these changes.

In summary, incident containment and rapid response are critical components of effective cybersecurity. They involve swift action to identify, contain, and mitigate security incidents to limit their impact on an organization. Having a well-defined incident response plan, a skilled incident response team, and the right technology tools in place are essential to successfully navigate the challenging landscape of cybersecurity threats. By prioritizing incident containment and rapid response, organizations can enhance their resilience and minimize the damage caused by security incidents.

Chapter 7: Offensive Security for Defensive Purposes

In the ever-evolving realm of cybersecurity, one of the most powerful and proactive tools at an organization's disposal is the practice of red team exercises and ethical hacking. These exercises serve as invaluable tools for identifying vulnerabilities, assessing security measures, and ultimately enhancing an organization's overall cybersecurity posture.

Red team exercises, often referred to as red teaming, are a structured and systematic approach to simulating cyberattacks. In these exercises, a group of skilled cybersecurity professionals, known as the red team, plays the role of adversaries attempting to breach an organization's defenses. The primary goal of the red team is to mimic real-world cyber threats, exploiting vulnerabilities and weaknesses in the organization's security measures.

Unlike conventional penetration testing, which typically focuses on identifying known vulnerabilities, red team exercises go a step further. Red teams employ a broader, more dynamic approach, emulating the tactics, techniques, and procedures (TTPs) of actual threat actors. This approach allows organizations to assess not only the robustness of their defenses but also their ability to detect and respond to sophisticated attacks.

Ethical hacking, often synonymous with penetration testing, is another essential component of an organization's cybersecurity strategy. Ethical hackers, also known as white hat hackers, are individuals or teams of experts who conduct controlled, authorized attacks on an organization's systems and networks to uncover vulnerabilities before malicious actors can exploit them.

The practice of ethical hacking involves a combination of manual testing and automated scanning to identify security weaknesses. These ethical hackers utilize the same tools and methodologies that malicious hackers might employ but with the explicit consent and engagement of the organization. Their aim is not to cause harm but to fortify the organization's defenses.

Together, red team exercises and ethical hacking encompass a broad range of activities aimed at evaluating an organization's security posture. These activities can include:

Network Penetration Testing: Simulating attacks on an organization's network infrastructure to identify vulnerabilities and security gaps.

Web Application Security Testing: Assessing the security of web applications, APIs, and websites to uncover vulnerabilities like SQL injection, cross-site scripting (XSS), and cross-site request forgery (CSRF).

Social Engineering Testing: Evaluating the effectiveness of security awareness and training programs by attempting to manipulate employees into divulging sensitive information or performing risky actions.

Phishing Simulations: Sending simulated phishing emails to employees to gauge their susceptibility to social engineering attacks.

Endpoint Security Testing: Assessing the security of individual devices, including workstations and mobile devices, to ensure they are properly configured and protected.

Wireless Security Testing: Evaluating the security of wireless networks, including Wi-Fi, to identify vulnerabilities and potential points of entry.

Physical Security Assessments: Testing the physical security of facilities, including access controls and surveillance systems.

The insights gained from red team exercises and ethical hacking are invaluable for organizations. They reveal vulnerabilities that may otherwise go unnoticed, providing a realistic assessment of an organization's security posture. By identifying weaknesses in advance, organizations can proactively address them, reducing the risk of data breaches, financial losses, and reputational damage.

It's important to emphasize that red team exercises and ethical hacking should always be conducted within a legal and ethical framework. Organizations should obtain proper authorization and consent before engaging in these activities to avoid any legal repercussions. Ethical hackers and red teams must adhere to strict rules of engagement and respect the boundaries defined by the organization.

Furthermore, the results of these exercises should be used constructively to improve cybersecurity measures. Organizations should take the findings seriously and prioritize remediation efforts based on the identified vulnerabilities. Regular assessments and continuous improvement are key to maintaining a strong security posture in the face of evolving cyber threats.

In summary, red team exercises and ethical hacking play pivotal roles in modern cybersecurity. They provide organizations with a proactive means of identifying vulnerabilities, testing security measures, and ultimately strengthening their defenses. By mimicking the tactics of real-world adversaries, ethical hackers and red teams offer a realistic assessment of an organization's readiness to face cyber threats. When conducted ethically and in compliance with legal standards, these exercises are powerful tools for enhancing cybersecurity in an increasingly digital and interconnected world.

In the realm of cybersecurity, the traditional approach to defense has predominantly been focused on building strong walls, implementing firewalls, intrusion detection systems, and antivirus software to keep threats at bay. However, as cyber threats continue to evolve and become more sophisticated, it has become increasingly clear that a purely defensive mindset may not be sufficient to protect against determined adversaries. This realization has led to a shift in the cybersecurity landscape, with organizations now exploring the concept of incorporating offensive tactics into their defense strategies.

One of the key drivers behind this shift is the recognition that defenders can benefit from adopting the mindset and tactics of offensive hackers, often referred to as "ethical hackers" or "white hat hackers." These cybersecurity professionals leverage their knowledge and skills to proactively identify vulnerabilities and weaknesses in an organization's systems and networks before malicious actors can exploit them.

By thinking like an attacker, ethical hackers can uncover security flaws and design weaknesses that may go unnoticed by traditional defensive measures. This proactive approach allows organizations to address vulnerabilities before they can be leveraged in a real-world cyberattack, reducing the risk of data breaches and other security incidents.

One common offensive tactic employed by ethical hackers is penetration testing. Penetration testing, often referred to as "pen testing," involves simulating cyberattacks against an organization's systems and networks to identify vulnerabilities and assess the effectiveness of security controls. Pen testers use a combination of manual testing and automated scanning tools to emulate the tactics of real-world attackers.

During a penetration test, ethical hackers may attempt to exploit vulnerabilities in web applications, network infrastructure, or even employee behaviors. The goal is to determine whether an attacker could successfully breach the organization's defenses and gain unauthorized access to sensitive data or systems. This valuable information can then be used to strengthen security measures and close security gaps.

Another offensive tactic that organizations can adopt for defensive purposes is red teaming. Red teaming involves the creation of a specialized team, often external to the organization, whose sole purpose is to simulate realistic cyberattacks. The red team operates independently and uses a wide range of tactics, techniques, and procedures (TTPs) to challenge an organization's defenses.

Red team exercises are typically more comprehensive and rigorous than traditional penetration tests, as they aim to assess an organization's overall readiness to detect and respond to sophisticated attacks. This includes evaluating the effectiveness of incident response processes, security monitoring capabilities, and the ability to thwart advanced persistent threats (APTs).

Incorporating offensive tactics into defense strategies also extends to the concept of threat hunting. Threat hunting is a proactive and iterative process that involves searching for signs of malicious activity within an organization's network, even in the absence of known indicators of compromise. Threat hunters use their expertise to identify anomalies, unusual behaviors, or subtle indicators that may suggest the presence of hidden threats.

By adopting a threat hunting mindset, organizations can actively seek out threats that may have evaded traditional security measures. This proactive approach can lead to the early detection and mitigation of cyber threats before they can cause significant damage.

Furthermore, organizations can leverage offensive tactics to assess the security awareness and preparedness of their employees. Social engineering tests, such as phishing simulations, can help identify potential weaknesses in employee training and awareness programs. Ethical hackers may craft convincing phishing emails or other social engineering attacks to gauge how employees respond and whether they follow security protocols.

While incorporating offensive tactics into defense strategies offers numerous advantages, it is essential to emphasize ethical and responsible conduct throughout the process. Organizations must conduct offensive activities within a legal and ethical framework, obtaining proper authorization and consent. Additionally, the results of penetration tests, red team exercises, and threat hunting should be used constructively to enhance security measures, rather than placing blame or punishment.

In summary, the incorporation of offensive tactics into defense strategies is a critical evolution in the field of cybersecurity. It reflects a proactive approach to identifying vulnerabilities, assessing security measures, and enhancing an organization's overall cybersecurity posture. By adopting the mindset and tactics of ethical hackers, organizations can better prepare themselves to defend against a wide range of cyber threats. Ultimately, the fusion of offensive and defensive cybersecurity practices empowers organizations to stay one step ahead of adversaries and protect their valuable assets in an increasingly complex threat landscape.

Chapter 8: Cloud Security and Defense

In today's digital landscape, the adoption of cloud computing has become a ubiquitous part of modern business operations, offering unparalleled scalability, flexibility, and cost-effectiveness. However, this transition to the cloud has also raised significant security concerns and challenges. Ensuring the security of data and applications in cloud environments is paramount, and that's where cloud security best practices and frameworks come into play.

Cloud security encompasses a broad range of practices, technologies, and policies designed to protect cloud-based resources and data from unauthorized access, data breaches, and cyber threats. With the ever-expanding use of cloud services and infrastructure, organizations must be well-versed in cloud security best practices to safeguard their digital assets effectively.

One fundamental aspect of cloud security is identity and access management (IAM). Properly managing and controlling user access to cloud resources is crucial. Organizations should implement robust IAM policies, ensuring that only authorized personnel can access sensitive data and applications. This includes multifactor authentication (MFA), strong password policies, and role-based access control (RBAC) to limit privileges based on job responsibilities.

Encryption is another critical element of cloud security. Data should be encrypted both in transit and at rest. Transport Layer Security (TLS) and Secure Sockets Layer (SSL) protocols are commonly used to encrypt data while it's transmitted over the internet. Additionally, cloud service providers often offer encryption options to protect data stored within their platforms, and organizations should take advantage of these features.

Regularly monitoring cloud environments is a best practice that cannot be overlooked. Security Information and Event Management (SIEM) solutions can help organizations detect and respond to security incidents in real-time. By continuously monitoring logs and events, suspicious activities can be identified and addressed promptly, minimizing potential damage.

Data backups and disaster recovery planning are essential components of cloud security. Organizations should implement robust backup and recovery strategies to ensure data resilience. This includes regularly backing up data and applications, storing backups in geographically diverse locations, and regularly testing recovery processes to confirm they are effective.

To address the unique challenges of cloud security, several industry-standard frameworks and best practice guides have emerged. One of the most widely recognized is the Cloud Security Alliance (CSA) Security Guidance. This comprehensive guide provides a detailed overview of cloud security best practices, covering everything from governance and risk management to compliance and incident response.

The Shared Responsibility Model is a concept often discussed in cloud security. It outlines the division of security responsibilities between cloud service providers (CSPs) and their customers. CSPs are responsible for securing the underlying cloud infrastructure, while customers are responsible for securing their data and applications within the cloud. Understanding this model is crucial for organizations to avoid security gaps.

Compliance with industry-specific regulations and standards is a top priority for many organizations. Whether it's the Health Insurance Portability and Accountability Act (HIPAA) for healthcare or the General Data Protection Regulation (GDPR) for data privacy, cloud security best practices must align with these requirements. Organizations should carefully assess their regulatory obligations and ensure that their cloud deployments meet compliance standards.

Containerization and microservices architecture have gained popularity in recent years, providing greater flexibility and scalability for cloud-based applications. However, they also introduce unique security challenges. Organizations should implement container security measures, such as vulnerability scanning, access control, and image signing, to protect containerized applications.

DevSecOps, a combination of development, security, and operations, has become a key approach to building security into the development process. By integrating security practices into the software development lifecycle, organizations can identify and address vulnerabilities early in the development process, reducing the risk of security incidents in production.

Zero Trust Security is a concept gaining traction in the cloud security landscape. It challenges the traditional perimeter-based security model and assumes that threats can come from both inside and outside the network. In a Zero Trust model, every user and device, whether inside or outside the corporate network, is verified and authenticated before being granted access to resources.

Cloud security best practices also extend to incident response and recovery planning. Organizations should develop clear incident response plans that outline how to detect, respond to, and recover from security incidents in a cloud environment. Regularly testing and updating these plans is essential to ensure their effectiveness.

The adoption of cloud security frameworks, such as the National Institute of Standards and Technology (NIST) Cybersecurity Framework or the Center for Internet Security (CIS) Controls, can provide organizations with a structured approach to securing their cloud environments. These frameworks offer guidelines and best practices for managing security risks.

In summary, cloud security is a multifaceted discipline that requires organizations to adopt a proactive and comprehensive approach to protect their digital assets. Cloud security best practices encompass identity and access management, encryption, monitoring, data backups, and disaster recovery. Understanding the Shared Responsibility Model and compliance requirements is essential, as is addressing the unique challenges posed by containerization and microservices. DevSecOps, Zero Trust Security, and robust incident response planning are all integral components of an effective cloud security strategy. By staying informed about emerging threats and adopting industry-standard frameworks, organizations can navigate the complexities of cloud security and safeguard their data and applications in the cloud.

In the ever-evolving landscape of cloud computing, organizations are increasingly adopting multi-cloud and hybrid cloud environments to meet their specific needs and requirements. While these cloud deployment models offer flexibility, scalability, and resilience, they also introduce unique security challenges that organizations must address effectively to protect their data and applications.

Multi-cloud environments involve the use of multiple cloud service providers to host different workloads, applications, or services. Hybrid cloud environments, on the other hand, combine both on-premises infrastructure and cloud services, allowing organizations to leverage the benefits of cloud while maintaining some level of control over their data and applications.

One of the primary challenges in securing multi-cloud and hybrid environments is maintaining consistent security policies and controls across different cloud providers and on-premises infrastructure. Each cloud service provider may have its own set of security tools, APIs, and configurations, making it essential for organizations to establish a unified security strategy that spans their entire IT ecosystem.

Identity and access management (IAM) is a critical component of securing multi-cloud and hybrid environments. Organizations should implement centralized IAM solutions to ensure that user access and privileges are consistently managed across all cloud and on-premises resources. This includes enforcing strong authentication methods, role-based access control (RBAC), and continuous monitoring of user activities.

Encryption plays a vital role in protecting data in transit and at rest within multi-cloud and hybrid environments. Organizations should leverage encryption solutions that are compatible with various cloud providers and on-premises systems to safeguard sensitive information effectively. Additionally, data encryption keys should be managed securely and independently from the cloud providers to maintain control over data access.

Monitoring and visibility are essential for detecting and responding to security incidents in multi-cloud and hybrid environments. Security Information and Event Management (SIEM) solutions and cloud-native monitoring tools can help organizations gain insights into their environment's security posture. Continuous monitoring of logs, events, and network traffic can help identify suspicious activities and potential threats.

Network security is another critical consideration in multi-cloud and hybrid environments. Organizations should implement robust network segmentation and firewall rules to isolate workloads and prevent unauthorized lateral movement within the network. Additionally, intrusion detection and prevention systems (IDPS) should be in place to detect and mitigate potential threats.

Cloud workload protection platforms (CWPP) and cloud security posture management (CSPM) tools are valuable additions to the security toolkit. CWPP solutions can provide real-time protection for cloud workloads by identifying and mitigating vulnerabilities and threats. CSPM tools help organizations assess their cloud configurations for security best practices and compliance with industry standards.

Compliance with regulatory requirements is a significant concern for organizations operating in multi-cloud and hybrid environments. Different cloud providers may have varying levels of compliance certifications and controls. To address this, organizations should carefully evaluate cloud providers' compliance offerings and ensure that their configurations and policies align with regulatory obligations.

Data governance and classification are crucial for managing data in multi-cloud and hybrid environments. Organizations should implement data classification policies to identify sensitive data and apply appropriate security controls. Data loss prevention (DLP) solutions can help monitor and protect data from unauthorized access and exfiltration. Containerization and microservices are increasingly being used in multi-cloud and hybrid environments to enhance application scalability and agility. However, securing containerized workloads and microservices presents unique challenges. Organizations should adopt container security best practices, including image scanning, runtime protection, and access control, to mitigate container-related risks. Threat detection and response capabilities should be an integral part of the security strategy in multi-cloud and hybrid environments. Organizations should establish incident response plans that outline procedures for identifying, mitigating, and recovering from security incidents. Regular tabletop exercises and incident simulations can help teams prepare for potential threats effectively.

Automation and orchestration play a significant role in maintaining security hygiene across multi-cloud and hybrid environments. Security policies and controls can be enforced consistently through automated workflows, reducing the risk of misconfigurations and human errors.

Vendor security assessments and due diligence are essential when selecting cloud service providers for multi-cloud deployments. Organizations should thoroughly evaluate the security practices, certifications, and incident response capabilities of their chosen providers to ensure they meet security requirements.

In summary, securing multi-cloud and hybrid environments is a multifaceted endeavor that requires careful planning, robust security controls, and a unified security strategy. Identity and access management, encryption, monitoring, network security, and compliance considerations should all be addressed to protect data and applications effectively. Embracing security technologies such as CWPP, CSPM, DLP, and container security tools can further enhance security posture. Additionally, proactive threat detection and response, automation, and vendor assessments are vital components of a comprehensive security approach in multi-cloud and hybrid environments.

Chapter 9: Insider Threat Detection and Mitigation

Understanding insider threats and effectively detecting them within an organization is paramount in today's cybersecurity landscape. An insider threat, unlike external threats, emanates from individuals within an organization who have privileged access and knowledge, making them a potent danger to an organization's data, systems, and reputation.

Identifying insider threat indicators and analyzing behavior patterns are critical components of an organization's security strategy. Insider threats can take various forms, ranging from intentional malicious actions to unintentional mistakes or negligence. Therefore, recognizing the signs and patterns associated with these threats is essential.

One of the key indicators of insider threats is a sudden change in an employee's behavior or work habits. An employee who suddenly starts accessing sensitive data or systems they haven't interacted with before might raise suspicion. Similarly, changes in work hours, accessing data outside regular business hours, or an increase in failed login attempts can all signal potential insider threats.

Monitoring an employee's access privileges is another vital aspect of insider threat detection. Frequent requests for elevated access or the granting of unnecessary privileges can indicate an insider's attempt to exploit their position. This can be especially concerning if these actions are not in line with an employee's job responsibilities.

Unusual data access patterns are significant red flags. For example, an employee who frequently downloads or copies large amounts of sensitive data, especially if it's data they don't typically need for their role, may be involved in malicious activity or data exfiltration. Analyzing data access logs can help identify such anomalies.

Changes in communication patterns can also provide insight into insider threats. An employee who suddenly starts communicating with unauthorized individuals or exhibits secretive behavior may be involved in activities detrimental to the organization's security. Monitoring email communications and other forms of digital communication can be instrumental in identifying suspicious behavior.

In some cases, disgruntled employees or those with a history of disciplinary issues may pose a higher risk of becoming insider threats. Tracking employee morale and addressing workplace grievances can help mitigate these risks and prevent potential security incidents.

Insider threats can manifest in various ways, from data theft to fraud or even sabotage. Detecting these threats often involves closely examining an employee's actions and intentions. For example, unauthorized attempts to modify or delete critical files, particularly if there's no legitimate reason for doing so, should raise alarms.

Employees with access to financial systems can pose significant insider threats. Unauthorized financial transactions, such as transferring funds to personal accounts or altering payment records, can result in financial losses for the organization. Regularly monitoring financial transactions and reconciling accounts can help uncover fraudulent activities.

In some cases, employees may exhibit signs of discontent or disgruntlement before engaging in malicious activities. It's essential for organizations to foster a positive work environment and encourage open communication to address employee concerns constructively and prevent potential insider threats.

Monitoring an employee's external activities can also be beneficial in detecting insider threats. This includes tracking an employee's online presence and identifying any suspicious or illegal activities outside of work that may indicate an increased risk of becoming an insider threat.

Collaborative efforts between HR and IT departments can enhance insider threat detection. HR can provide valuable insights into employee behavior, while IT can implement monitoring and auditing mechanisms to track and analyze digital activities. By combining these efforts, organizations can identify potential insider threats more effectively.

Behavioral analytics and machine learning can play a pivotal role in insider threat detection. These technologies can analyze vast amounts of data to identify unusual patterns and flag potential threats. For example, an employee accessing sensitive data at irregular times or locations could trigger an alert based on behavioral analysis.

Insider threats can also stem from unintentional actions, such as falling victim to phishing attacks. Employees who inadvertently click on malicious links or download infected files can unknowingly introduce security risks. Therefore, providing cybersecurity training and awareness programs is crucial to reducing the likelihood of insider threats originating from unwitting employees.

Employee monitoring tools, while essential for threat detection, should be implemented carefully to respect privacy and legal regulations. Organizations must strike a balance between monitoring for security purposes and preserving employees' privacy rights. Clear policies and communication regarding monitoring practices are essential.

In summary, recognizing insider threat indicators and analyzing behavior patterns is a fundamental aspect of modern cybersecurity. Insider threats can take various forms, and detecting them requires a combination of monitoring employee behavior, access privileges, data access patterns, communication habits, and external activities. Leveraging technology, such as behavioral analytics and machine learning, can enhance the effectiveness of insider threat detection efforts. Additionally, fostering a positive work environment, providing cybersecurity training, and implementing clear monitoring policies are essential components of a comprehensive strategy to mitigate insider threats and protect an organization's assets and reputation.

Implementing effective insider threat mitigation programs is crucial for organizations seeking to protect their data, systems, and reputation. These programs aim to detect, prevent, and respond to insider threats effectively, reducing the risks associated with malicious or unintentional actions by employees or trusted individuals. Next, we will explore the key components and strategies for implementing insider threat mitigation programs.

The first step in establishing an insider threat mitigation program is to define clear objectives and goals. Organizations should have a comprehensive understanding of what they aim to achieve through the program, whether it's reducing the frequency of insider incidents, minimizing the impact of insider threats, or both. These objectives will guide the development of strategies and tactics.

One of the foundational elements of an insider threat mitigation program is creating policies and procedures that address insider threats specifically. These policies should outline acceptable use of organizational resources, data access privileges, and behavioral expectations. Employees should be made aware of these policies and understand the consequences of violating them.

Training and awareness programs play a critical role in educating employees about insider threats and best practices for preventing them. These programs should cover various aspects, including recognizing phishing attempts, safeguarding sensitive data, and reporting suspicious activities. Regular training sessions and awareness campaigns help keep employees informed and vigilant.

Implementing access controls is essential to limit the potential for insider threats. Organizations should adopt the principle of least privilege, ensuring that employees only have access to the data and systems necessary for their roles. Access should be regularly reviewed and adjusted as job responsibilities change.

User monitoring and auditing are key components of insider threat mitigation. Organizations should deploy tools and systems to monitor user activities, including data access, network traffic, and system logins. Regular audits of these logs can help identify suspicious behavior and deviations from normal usage patterns.

User behavior analytics (UBA) and anomaly detection technologies can provide valuable insights into insider threat activities. These solutions analyze user behavior and flag deviations from established baselines. For example, if an employee suddenly accesses a large volume of sensitive data or logs in from an unusual location, UBA can generate alerts.

Effective communication channels for reporting insider threats should be established within the organization. Employees should feel comfortable reporting suspicious activities without fear of retaliation. These reporting mechanisms can include anonymous hotlines, email addresses, or designated personnel responsible for handling insider threat reports.

Incident response plans specific to insider threats should be developed and tested regularly. These plans outline the steps to be taken in the event of an insider threat incident, including containment, investigation, and mitigation. Testing ensures that the response team is well-prepared to handle insider threats effectively.

Insider threat programs should involve collaboration between various departments, including HR, IT, legal, and security. HR can provide insights into employee behavior, while IT and security teams can implement technical controls and monitoring solutions. Legal guidance is essential to navigate legal and regulatory aspects of insider threat investigations.

Continuous monitoring of employee morale and job satisfaction is important in identifying potential insider threats. Dissatisfaction or grievances can lead to disgruntled employees who may be more susceptible to engaging in malicious activities. Addressing workplace issues promptly can prevent potential insider threats.

Implementing a robust data loss prevention (DLP) strategy is crucial for safeguarding sensitive information. DLP solutions can monitor and block the unauthorized transfer or sharing of sensitive data, preventing insider threats from exfiltrating valuable information.

Regularly reviewing and updating insider threat mitigation strategies is essential to stay ahead of evolving threats. Threat landscapes change, and insider threat programs must adapt accordingly. Conducting threat assessments and risk analyses can help organizations identify new risks and vulnerabilities.

Privacy considerations should be a priority when implementing insider threat mitigation programs. Organizations must strike a balance between security and respecting employees' privacy rights. Clearly defined policies and transparent communication can help address these concerns.

In summary, implementing insider threat mitigation programs requires a multi-faceted approach that encompasses policies, training, access controls, monitoring, incident response, and collaboration between departments. By establishing clear objectives, educating employees, and deploying the right technology and processes, organizations can significantly reduce the risks associated with insider threats. Regularly reviewing and adapting these programs ensures their continued effectiveness in an ever-changing threat landscape.

Chapter 10: Securing Critical Infrastructure and IoT

In today's increasingly connected world, the Internet of Things (IoT) has become ubiquitous, revolutionizing various aspects of our daily lives. The proliferation of IoT devices, ranging from smart thermostats and fitness trackers to industrial sensors and autonomous vehicles, has brought numerous benefits, including convenience and efficiency. However, this interconnected ecosystem also presents significant security challenges and vulnerabilities that must be addressed comprehensively. One of the primary challenges in IoT security is the sheer scale and diversity of IoT devices. These devices vary in terms of their manufacturers, operating systems, and communication protocols, making it challenging to implement consistent security measures across the board. Moreover, many IoT devices are resource-constrained, with limited computing power and memory, which can hinder the implementation of robust security features. This limitation can leave IoT devices vulnerable to attacks that leverage their resource constraints to bypass security mechanisms.

Another significant vulnerability in IoT security is the potential for unauthorized access. IoT devices often collect and transmit sensitive data, making them attractive targets for malicious actors seeking to steal personal information, compromise privacy, or launch cyberattacks. Weak or default credentials, insufficient authentication mechanisms, and inadequate encryption can all contribute to unauthorized access and data breaches. Furthermore, IoT devices are frequently deployed in physically accessible environments, making them susceptible to tampering or theft. IoT devices often rely on wireless communication protocols to connect to networks and other devices. While wireless connectivity enables flexibility and mobility, it also introduces security risks. For instance, eavesdropping, jamming, and spoofing attacks can disrupt communications and compromise the integrity and confidentiality of data transmitted by IoT devices. Insecure wireless communication can also expose IoT devices to man-in-the-middle attacks, where an attacker intercepts and manipulates data exchanged between the device and its intended recipient. Inadequate firmware and software security is another critical vulnerability in IoT ecosystems. Manufacturers may release IoT devices with outdated or vulnerable firmware that lacks security patches. Additionally, IoT devices often have a long lifespan, which means that security updates may not be consistently available or applied. This can leave devices exposed to known vulnerabilities for extended periods, increasing the risk of exploitation. Insecure over-the-air (OTA) update mechanisms can also be targeted by attackers to compromise IoT device firmware.

Many IoT ecosystems involve third-party services and cloud platforms for data storage, processing, and analysis. While these services offer scalability and convenience, they introduce potential security risks. Inadequate security measures on cloud servers can lead to data breaches and unauthorized access to IoT device data. Moreover, the reliance on external services can raise concerns about data privacy and ownership. IoT devices are often integrated into larger systems, such as industrial control systems and critical infrastructure. Compromising an IoT device within these systems can have far-reaching consequences, including disruptions to essential services and infrastructure. Attackers may exploit vulnerabilities in IoT devices to gain a foothold in larger networks or launch coordinated attacks. The complexity of IoT ecosystems can make it challenging to detect and respond to security incidents promptly. Traditional security monitoring tools and approaches may not be well-suited to the unique characteristics and behaviors of IoT devices. IoT devices can generate vast amounts of data, making it difficult to distinguish between normal and suspicious activities. Furthermore, IoT devices may exhibit unconventional communication patterns, making anomaly detection more complex. The lack of standardized security practices and regulations for IoT devices further complicates the security landscape. Manufacturers may prioritize functionality and time-to-market over security, resulting in devices with inadequate protections. While some regions have introduced IoT security regulations, the global nature of IoT presents challenges for enforcement and compliance. Interoperability among IoT devices can also introduce security risks. Devices from different manufacturers may need to communicate and share data, but compatibility issues can lead to security vulnerabilities. This interconnectivity can create complex attack surfaces, as compromising one device may provide a path to infiltrate an entire network. The expanding attack surface introduced by IoT devices presents a significant challenge for organizations seeking to defend against cyber threats. As the number of IoT devices within an organization grows, so does the potential entry points for attackers. This necessitates a shift in security strategies towards proactive risk management and threat prevention. Organizations must implement comprehensive security measures that encompass device authentication, encryption, access control, and regular software updates. In addition to protecting IoT devices themselves, securing the network infrastructure and cloud services supporting IoT ecosystems is paramount.

Network segmentation, intrusion detection systems, and encryption of data in transit can enhance overall IoT security. Security awareness and training for both employees and end-users are essential components of IoT security. Users should be educated on best practices for securing IoT devices, such as changing default passwords, keeping firmware up to date, and being cautious about sharing sensitive information. Employees responsible for managing IoT deployments should receive specialized training to address IoT-specific security challenges. Security standards and frameworks specific to IoT can provide valuable guidance for organizations. These standards can help establish baseline security requirements and best practices for IoT device manufacturers, service providers, and end-users. Examples of IoT security standards include the IoT Cybersecurity Improvement Act and the IoT Security Foundation's best practice guidelines. IoT security is an ongoing process that requires collaboration among stakeholders, including device manufacturers, service providers, regulators, and end-users. As the IoT landscape continues to evolve, addressing security challenges and vulnerabilities must remain a top priority to ensure the continued growth and success of IoT technologies. By adopting a proactive and collaborative approach to IoT security, organizations can minimize risks and enjoy the benefits of a connected and efficient future. Critical infrastructure refers to the essential systems and assets, both physical and virtual, that are vital to the functioning of a society and its economy.

These critical infrastructure elements include energy production and distribution, water supply, transportation networks, communication systems, and more.

Ensuring the protection and resilience of critical infrastructure is a paramount concern for governments and organizations worldwide.

The importance of critical infrastructure lies in its role as the backbone of modern society, enabling the delivery of essential services and supporting economic activities.

The disruption or compromise of critical infrastructure can have far-reaching and devastating consequences, affecting public safety, national security, and economic stability.

The protection of critical infrastructure involves a multidisciplinary approach that encompasses physical security, cybersecurity, risk management, and resilience planning.

Physical security measures for critical infrastructure include access controls, surveillance systems, and perimeter defenses to deter and prevent unauthorized access.

These measures are essential to safeguarding facilities like power plants, water treatment plants, and transportation hubs.

In addition to physical security, cybersecurity plays a crucial role in protecting critical infrastructure.

The increasing digitization of infrastructure systems has made them vulnerable to cyberattacks, which can disrupt operations, steal sensitive data, or even cause physical damage.

Cybersecurity measures include network monitoring, intrusion detection, and robust incident response capabilities.

Risk management is an integral part of critical infrastructure protection.

Identifying vulnerabilities and assessing potential threats help organizations and governments prioritize resources and efforts to protect infrastructure effectively.

Risk assessments also guide the development of mitigation strategies to address vulnerabilities and reduce the impact of potential threats.

Resilience planning is a key aspect of critical infrastructure protection, focusing on the ability to withstand and recover from disruptions.

Resilience involves redundancies, backup systems, and disaster recovery plans to ensure that critical services can be quickly restored after an incident.

Collaboration and information sharing are critical components of critical infrastructure protection.

Governments, private-sector organizations, and international bodies must work together to identify emerging threats, share threat intelligence, and coordinate responses to incidents.

Public-private partnerships play a significant role in enhancing the security and resilience of critical infrastructure.

Government agencies and private companies collaborate to share information, resources, and expertise to protect vital systems.

The U.S. Department of Homeland Security's Critical Infrastructure Partnership Advisory Council (CIPAC) is an example of such a partnership.

International cooperation is also essential in addressing the global nature of critical infrastructure threats.

Cyberattacks and physical attacks on critical infrastructure can have transnational implications, necessitating cooperation between nations to combat these threats effectively.

The United Nations and organizations like INTERPOL facilitate international collaboration on critical infrastructure protection.

As technology continues to advance, critical infrastructure protection faces new challenges.

The emergence of the Internet of Things (IoT) and the integration of digital technologies into infrastructure systems create new entry points for potential threats.

Ensuring the security of IoT devices and the networks they connect to is a critical concern.

In addition, the increasing interconnectivity of critical infrastructure systems poses both opportunities and risks.

While interconnected systems can enhance efficiency and effectiveness, they also create pathways for cascading failures if one system is compromised.

Therefore, robust cybersecurity measures and segmentation of critical systems are vital to prevent the spread of disruptions.

Another challenge in critical infrastructure protection is the evolving threat landscape.

Nation-states, cybercriminal organizations, hacktivists, and other threat actors are continually developing new tactics and tools.

Staying ahead of these threats requires ongoing monitoring, threat intelligence sharing, and adaptation of security measures.

Climate change introduces additional challenges to critical infrastructure protection.

Extreme weather events, such as hurricanes, floods, and wildfires, can damage or destroy infrastructure components.

Organizations and governments must incorporate climate resilience into their planning to ensure infrastructure can withstand and recover from these events.

Innovations in technology, such as artificial intelligence (AI) and machine learning, have the potential to enhance critical infrastructure protection.

These technologies can improve threat detection, automate responses, and analyze vast amounts of data for anomalies.

However, they also raise ethical and privacy concerns that must be addressed.

Public awareness and engagement are vital aspects of critical infrastructure protection.

Educating the public about the importance of protecting critical infrastructure and encouraging reporting of suspicious activities can enhance security efforts.

Infrastructure owners and operators must also engage with their local communities to build trust and cooperation.

In summary, critical infrastructure protection is an ongoing and multifaceted effort that requires collaboration, risk management, and resilience planning. Protecting essential systems and assets is essential for the well-being of society and the stability of economies. By addressing physical security, cybersecurity, risk management, and resilience, organizations and governments can mitigate threats and ensure the continued functioning of critical infrastructure.

Conclusion

In this comprehensive book bundle, "Blue Team Operations: Defense," we've explored the essential principles and practices that form the foundation of an effective blue team. From operational security to incident response and digital forensics, these four books provide a holistic view of the strategies and techniques required to defend against modern cyber threats. In "Blue Team Essentials: A Beginner's Guide to Operational Security," readers learned the fundamental concepts of operational security, including threat modeling, risk assessment, and secure communication practices. This book served as an excellent starting point for those new to the world of blue team operations. "Mastering Incident Response: Strategies for Blue Teams" delved into the art of incident response, covering everything from developing an incident response plan to executing effective investigations and recovery processes. It equipped blue teams with the skills needed to rapidly detect, analyze, and mitigate security incidents. Our third book, "Digital Forensics for Blue Teams: Advanced Techniques and Investigations," took readers into the world of digital forensics, exploring advanced methods for collecting and analyzing digital evidence. This book provided the knowledge and tools necessary to conduct in-depth investigations, aiding blue teams in uncovering the truth behind security incidents. The final installment, "Expert Blue Team Operations: Defending Against Advanced Threats," elevated readers' understanding of blue team operations to an advanced level. It covered topics such as threat hunting, threat intelligence, and tactics for defending against sophisticated adversaries. Throughout this book bundle, we emphasized the importance of collaboration, information sharing, and continuous learning within the blue team community. As cyber threats continue to evolve, the role of blue teams in defending organizations becomes increasingly critical. In summary, "Blue Team Operations: Defense" offers a comprehensive and practical resource for those looking to enhance their skills in operational security, incident response, and digital forensics. Whether you're a beginner or an experienced professional, this bundle provides valuable insights and techniques to help you protect your organization against the ever-changing landscape of cyber threats. We hope that the knowledge gained from these books will empower blue teams to adapt and excel in their mission of safeguarding digital assets and preserving the integrity of information systems.